YO-ABR-394

Managed Care in American Indian and Alaska Native Communities

MIM DIXON

AMERICAN PUBLIC HEALTH ASSOCIATION

American Public Health Association
1015 Fifteenth St., NW
Washington, DC 20005-2605

Mohammad N. Akhter, MD, MPH
Executive Director

5.5 M 11/98
Library of Congress Catalog Card Number: 98-74063

ISBN: 0-87553-238-1

Printed and bound in the United States of America.
Cover Design: Sam Dixon
Book Design and Typesetting: Jean-Marie Navetta, APHA
Set in: Goudy and Optima
Printing and Binding: United Book Press

Table of Contents

Acknowledgments

This project would not have been possible without the sponsorship of the National Indian Health Board and the participation of Tribes and urban Indian programs. I would like to thank Tanana Chiefs Conference, Inc., the Pascua Yaqui Tribe, the Indian Health Board of Minneapolis, and the Mashantucket Pequot Tribal Nation for agreeing to participate in this study.

At each of these case study sites, there have been one or two individuals who took responsibility for planning my visit, arranging interviews, and assembling written documents for my review. Their assistance enabled me to gather information in an efficient and comprehensive way. So, I extend a special thanks to Merlan O. Ellis at Tanana Chiefs Conference, Inc.; Jack Rameriz at Pascua Yaqui, whose untimely death has saddened all who knew him; Carol Marquez and Virginia Schuster at the Indian Health Board of Minneapolis, and George McMullen and Mike Sockalexis at the Mashantucket Pequot Tribal Nation. Through these coordinators, I was able to interview dozens of people. A list of those who gave generously of their time and information is at the end of this report.

A very knowledgeable Advisory Committee helped to guide this project and review drafts of the report. They included Terry

Batliner, DDS, Network Director, Veterans Health Administration; Leigh Brown, JD, Associate Director, Oklahoma Health Care Authority; Helen Collins, Health Insurance Specialist, Health Care Financing Administration; Merlan O. Ellis, RN, Director of Contract Health Services, Chief Andrew Isaac Health Center; James R. Floyd, Director, Portland Area Office Indian Health Service; Annette Menihan, Director of Tribal Health and Human Services Department and Vice Chair of the Pequot Pharmaceutical Network, Mashantucket Pequot Tribal Nation; Jack Rameriz, Health Plan Manager, Pascua Yaqui Tribe; Norine Smith, Executive Director, Indian Health Board of Minneapolis; and Alex Trujillo, Associate Regional Administrator, Health Care Financing Administration.

Thanks are extended to the Henry J. Kaiser Family Foundation, which offered insights and ideas through the project officers Pancho Chang, JD, and Vice President Michael Sinclair, PhD.

My thanks go to the American Public Health Association Publications Board and staff. Berttina Wentworth, MD, and Dorothy S. Oda, DNSc, provided encouragement and helpful reviews of draft manuscripts. Thanks also are extended to Ellen T. Meyer, Director of Publications.

My colleagues at the National Indian Health Board provided valuable assistance, including Brenda Shore and Rosalie Tallbull. I especially appreciate the vision and enthusiastic support of Executive Director Yvette Joseph-Fox, MSW.

Mim Dixon

List of Abbreviations

AFA   Annual Funding Agreement
AFDC   Aid to Families with Dependent Children
AHCCCS   Arizona Health Care Cost Containment System
ALTCS   Arizona Long Term Care System
ANCSA   Alaska Native Claims Settlement Act
ANMC   Alaska Native Medical Center
BAH   Bassett Army Hospital
BIA   Bureau of Indian Affairs
CAIHC   Chief Andrew Isaac Health Center
CHA   Community Health Aide
CHEF   Catastrophic Health Emergency Fund
CHS   Contract Health Service
CPA   Certified public accountant
EAP   Employee Assistance Program
ECP   Essential community provider
EHS   Employee Health Services
ERISA   Employee Retirement Income Security Act of 1974
EVS   Electronic Verification System
FARxNET   First American Pharmaceutical Network
FFS   Fee for service
FMH   Fairbanks Memorial Hospital
FQHC   Federally Qualified Health Center

GA   General Assistance
GAMC   General Assistance Medical Care
HCFA   Health Care Financing Administration
HCMC   Hennepin County Medical Center
HFA   Hennepin Faculty Associates
HMO   Health Maintenance Organization
IBNR   Incurred but not reported
IHB   Indian Health Board
IHS   Indian Health Service
IMBF   Indian Member Benefit Fund
IPA   Independent Practice Association
IPO   Independent Practice Organizations
JCAHO   Joint Commission on Accreditation
of Healthcare Organizations
MA   Medical Assistance
MCO   Managed care organization
MHP   Metropolitan Health Plan
MOA   Memorandum of Agreement
MPHBP   Mashantucket Pequot Health Benefit Plan
MPTN   Mashantucket Pequot Tribal Nation
NACHC   National Association of Community Health Centers
OB/GYN   Obstetrician and gynecologist
PCP   Primary Care Provider
PHS   Physician Health Services
PIMC   Phoenix Indian Medical Center
PMAP   Prepaid Medical Assistance Program
PMG   Participating Medical Group

POS-PPO Point of Service Preferred Provider Organization
PPO Preferred Provider Organization
PRxN Pequot Pharmaceutical Network
QA Quality assurance
QA/UR Quality assurance/utilization review
RFP Request for proposals
RPMS Resource and Patient Management System
SOBRA Sixth Omnibus Budget Reconciliation Act
SSI Supplemental Security Income
TANF Temporary Assistance to Needy Families
TCC Tanana Chiefs Conference, Inc.
TPA Third-party administrator
USET United South and Eastern Tribes
WIC Women, Infants and Children's nutrition program

Preface

As managed care sweeps the country, it is touching the lives of some of the most culturally distinct people living in both the most remote rural areas and the most impoverished inner cities—American Indians and Alaska Natives. Looking at how managed care affects the delivery of health services to Native Americans may provide insights about how managed care could affect other minority populations. Furthermore, the Indian Health Service has developed a unique federal health care system with an emphasis on public health. Thus, public health professionals may find the examples of managed care in this study relevant to their diverse missions.

There are 556 federally recognized Tribes in the United States. These are the political organizations for more than 2 million American Indian and Alaska Native people. Treaties and laws between the United States and the Indian Nations define a special relationship that acknowledges a federal trust responsibility, as well as a government-to-government relationship between the federal government and Tribes. The federal trust responsibility for health care for Native Americans is administered primarily through the Indian Health Service within the U.S. Public Health Service, a division of the Department of Health and Human Services. However, all federal agencies are expected to engage in government-to-government consultations with federally recognized tribes.

Native Americans are one of the smallest minority populations in the country, so the cost of their health care is a tiny fraction of the amount needed to provide health services to the whole of the nation. In addition to the benefits they receive through the Indian Health Service, American Indian and Alaska Native people are entitled to participate in programs designed to serve broader groups of minority populations. Those who meet the eligibility qualification for Medicaid and state medical assistance programs are also entitled to those benefits. Given the small size of the Native American population and the number of programs which could be providing health care, it is surprising that American Indians and Alaska Natives are among the most medically underserved and have the poorest health of any group in our country.

As Indian people are taking control of the management of their own health care delivery systems, they are achieving some remarkable results in reducing costs, while increasing the scope of benefits and improving the quality of care. Their complex political and economic environment includes managed care. While this book is written to help Native American people understand the concepts of managed care and the opportunities and challenges it presents, this same information may be useful to other planners and administrators who are attempting to grapple with changes resulting from managed care. While the examples are presented here in the context of Indian health care delivery systems, it is hoped that they will help illuminate a complex subject for those working outside the Native American communities, as well as for those working for Tribes.

As most state Medicaid programs move toward managed care, Native American populations are such a small part of their constituency that they are often forgotten. As managed care organizations grow larger and more national in scope, they can hardly bother to negotiate with small tribal and urban Indian health providers. In the huge federal bureaucracy of the Health Care Financing Administration, advocacy for Indian issues is among the lowest priorities. At the same time, these large organizations are having a huge impact on the health care for American Indian and Alaska Native people. It is hoped that the vantage point provided in this book will help organizations in the managed care arena to better understand the perspectives and goals of Native Americans.

Chapter 1

Introduction

These case studies of managed care in Indian health settings are intended to introduce Tribes to the basic concepts of managed care and help them visualize ways to take advantage of opportunities that managed care presents.

Tribes serve many roles related to health care. They advocate for services on behalf of tribal members. They provide health services under contracts or annual funding agreements with the Indian Health Service (IHS), often with additional funding from Medicaid and other third parties. They may manage a Contract Health Services program in which they purchase health services from the private sector. They may purchase a health benefit package for tribal employees. In every role, managed care is providing both opportunities and challenges for Tribes.

In the private sector, managed care has emerged in the past decade as an alternative to health insurance and the fee-for-service system of paying health care providers. More than 70 percent of employees who have health benefits are now enrolled in managed care plans. In the past, these employees had indemnity plans, or health insurance. In the past, they would go to the doctor of their choice, pay the bill, and submit a claim to the insurance company which would likely reimburse them for 80 percent of customary charges after they met the required deductible. Today, employees enrolled in managed care plans must select a primary care provider from a network of providers offered by the plan. When the consumer goes to the doctor, they typically pay a flat fee of about $10, called a "copay." The doctor is usually paid a fixed amount per patient per month by the health plan.

Because managed care has proven its ability to control costs of health benefits paid by employers, it has become an attractive approach for government programs which also are seeking predictable, stable expenditures. In the past three years, many states have changed their Medicaid programs from fee-for-service to managed care. Because most Indian health programs rely on Medicaid reimbursements as a significant portion of their budgets, they have encountered many challenges in adapting to the new managed care environment.

Remember the childhood story of "The Blind Men and the Elephant"? Each blind man touches a different part of the elephant and each describes a different kind of animal. While each of the descriptions is different from the others, all of them are right. Taken together they describe the whole animal. These case studies are like the Blind Men and the Elephant. Managed care is like the huge animal that seems different from different angles. Consumers, providers, plans and purchasers are like the blind men, each with a different perspective on managed care. To understand managed care, we need to look at it from different angles.

What Is Managed Care?

Managed care is a term for all types of integrated health care delivery systems. There are four essential components to managed care: a purchaser, a health plan, providers, and consumers.

- The purchaser, usually an employer or a state Medicaid program, pays for the plan.
- The health plan is both an organization and a document that defines benefits and costs. Health plans are also called managed care organizations (MCOs) and health maintenance organizations (HMOs). As an organization, the plan receives money from the purchaser and uses it to pay the providers for services to the consumers. Managing money is the main goal of the plan. Contractual relationships define a network of providers within the plan.
- Providers are doctors, hospitals, laboratories, home health agencies, and others who deliver health services to consumers.

- Consumers enroll as members of the plan and receive
  services from providers in the plan's network according to the rules of the plan.

As these case studies illustrate, Indian health organizations can serve in any of these roles.

Managed care includes a variety of approaches for organizing the delivery of health services, which usually share
the following features:

1. A health plan defines benefits and limitations for the consumer at a fixed annual cost.

In the private sector, a managed care health plan has
replaced the traditional insurance policy as the way of receiving money from the purchaser and paying health care
providers for services. In the past, most employers who provided health benefits would purchase insurance policies for
their employees and the insurance policy would pay claims
to a provider. Today, a growing number of employers pay a
fixed amount for employees to enroll in managed care health
plans. Enrollment in a health plan means that the health plan
members have access to all the services listed in the plan;
however, they have to obtain those services from designated
providers according to the rules of the health plan. With
most traditional health insurance policies, people had the
freedom to choose their own providers and to obtain most
any service they felt they needed. In health plans, members
are restricted to providers listed in the health plan, and those

providers decide what services are needed. For both insurance and health plans, there is a fixed annual cost. However, the costs for consumers are more predictable for managed care plans than for traditional insurance.

2. Health care providers are part of networks organized by health plans and defined by their contractual relationships with the plan.

With insurance policies, doctors could work in private, independent practices and simply bill insurance companies for the services they provide. Managed care plans organize networks of providers, usually including both doctors and hospitals, which are linked through contractual relationships. These contracts define payment processes, practice policies, and referral networks. Contracts can limit doctors to prescribing medicines from a formulary (a list of acceptable drugs under the health plan), require them to refer patients only to other doctors who also are linked contractually to the health plan, stipulate the hospitals where they can admit patients, and require reporting from the physicians.

3. Primary care providers are generally paid a fixed amount for each patient assigned to their care.

Under the historical fee-for-service approach, the costs are paid for each service actually delivered, regardless of the number of visits to a provider or the number of procedures in any single visit. The managed care approach usually pays the same amount for each member enrolled each month, regardless of whether extensive services or no services were delivered. Managed care is like the maintenance agreements that people purchase for their cars or refrigerators. With these maintenance agreements, a fixed amount is prepaid. If anything breaks, the company must provide service and fix it regardless of the cost. In managed care, the cost per patient per month is called the "capitation rate."

4. Financial risk usually is shared by the providers.

With traditional insurance policies, the more services doctors provided, the more they were paid. Under that system, the insurance companies carried all the risk of losing money because they had to pay the claims. However, when managed care provides a fixed payment per patient per month, the doctors are at risk of losing money if their costs are greater than their capitated income. This gives doctors an incentive to keep patient care costs low. The idea of managed care is that doctors will practice better medicine and keep patients healthier if they share in the financial risk. As with a maintenance agreement on a wash machine, the company has an incentive to do preventive maintenance because it is usually cheaper to prevent a problem than to fix it. Managed care is designed on the same concept. If doctors practice prevention (such as immunizations and health education), early detection (such as cancer screening) and health maintenance monitoring (such as regular appointments for people with diabetes and heart disease), it will cost them less than if they wait to treat diseases which have gotten very complicated.

Assuming risk through capitated payments usually requires a very large pool of patients. It is expected that some patients will be healthy while others may be sick. Sick patients may require services more costly than the capitation rate. However, capitated income from healthy patients usually gives the provider enough money to cover the costs of sick patients. If the pool of patients for a provider is too small, it is unfair to ask the provider to assume risk because there may not be sufficient healthy patients to make a profit. Therefore, these providers are usually paid a fee for service.

5. Total risk is limited through reinsurance or stop-loss plans.

Most managed care health plans take steps to protect themselves from losses that cannot be controlled through usual practice guidelines. For example, a premature birth can lead to excessive costs for prolonged neonatal intensive care, surgery, and related services. To protect themselves from these types of excessive costs, most health plans and/or providers purchase a type of insurance product from private insurance companies which starts at a relatively high level of costs. Another alternative for health plans or providers that are large enough to create a reserve pool of funds is to establish a self-insurance program to limit the cost of reinsurance. A third alternative is for health plans to provide this type of insurance for the providers in their network.

Stop-loss insurance coverage may be purchased by a health plan or provider to provide protection from losses resulting from claims over a specific dollar amount per member per year. There are two types of stop-loss insurance: specific or individual, and aggregate. For specific or individual insurance coverage, reimbursement is given for claims on any covered individual which exceed a predetermined deductible, such as $25,000 or $50,000. Aggregate insurance reimburses claims in which the total exceeds a predetermined level, such as 125 percent of the amount expected in an average year.

6. Case management, preadmission screening, utilization review, formularies and copayments are used to provide services in the most economical way.

Managed care is about both managing health care and managing money. Several strategies are used to accomplish both of these goals, including case management, preadmission screening, utilization review, and copayments.

There are two basic aspects of case management. One is managing patient care to keep patients healthy. This includes systems for assuring that prevention, screening, and health maintenance monitoring are implemented. The other is treating patients in the least costly way to meet their health care needs. For example, it is less expensive to provide health services by a primary care provider or midlevel practitioner (nurse practitioner or physician assistant) than to provide health services by a specialist. In many managed care systems, both aspects of case management are handled by assigning each health plan member to a primary care provider who is responsible for managing the member's health care. These primary care providers serve as "gatekeepers." This means that health plan members cannot see specialists unless they are referred by a primary care provider. Thus, primary care providers can assure that consumers receive appropriate, coordinated, family-based care.

Preadmission screenings help providers make decisions that lead to the most cost-effective care. For example, it is less expensive to provide outpatient surgery when appropriate than to hospitalize the patient for surgery. Decisions made during preadmission screening are usually based on recognized standards of care. This approach also protects consumers from unnecessary surgeries.

Utilization review and discharge planning are tools to monitor the length of stay for hospital patients and reduce hospital costs by sending patients to less expensive settings, such as nursing homes or their places of residence, as soon as it is safe to do so. Utilization review compares the patient's length of stay in the hospital with the average length of stay for most patients with the same diagnosis or proce-

dures. Preadmission screening may authorize a certain number of days in the hospital. Utilization review then requires
doctors to justify additional hospital days.

Discharge planning helps to assure that there is continuity of care after the patient leaves the hospital. Purchasers of plans may help define criteria that recognize local
preferences, such as length of stay in the hospital after a
delivery. Home health services assist patients after they leave
the hospital. Many tribes provide community-based services,
such as public health nurses and community health representatives who make home visits. Some Tribes have found
that these services can be managed to meet the criteria for
home health care and Medicare and other third parties will
pay for these services because they reduce the length of stay
in hospitals or nursing homes.

Health plans try to fill prescriptions in the most economical way. For some health plans, this includes formularies, which are a list of medicines that physicians may
prescribe under a plan. For many types of medicines, there
are several manufacturers offering the same drug under
different names at different costs. Formularies seek to give
physicians the flexibility to treat common problems with
different doses of the medicine that is most economical. By
using generic drugs rather than brand names and limiting
inventories, health plans can save money.

In a fee-for-service setting, patients are often charged a
deductible (an amount they must pay before the insurance

begins coverage) and a percentage of the charge for a service. In managed care, health plan members often make a contribution before the service is delivered through a payroll deduction and pay a small charge for specific services. These charges are called "copayments" or "copays." Copays are a fixed amount (such as $10 per visit) rather than a percentage of costs. These charges provide an incentive to reduce unnecessary utilization of high-cost services. For example, a copay for an emergency room visit is usually significantly more than a copay for a visit to the doctor's office. Providers of IHS-funded services to IHS-eligible patients cannot charge a copay.

7. Costs are controlled through a variety of measures, such as discounts in contracts with providers and group purchasing through networks.

While some managed care is offered through a single organization, most health plans contract with many organizations. The single organization approach is usually called a staff model HMO. Plans that include many organizations usually contract with groups of physicians called independent practice associations (IPAs) or participating medical groups (PMGs). A single IPA or PMG may contract with many different health plans, just as a physician may have patients with many different kinds of health insurance. When a health plan contracts with providers, the health plan negotiates rates. Providers are expected to offer lower negotiated rates in exchange for a higher volume of patients.

Because health plans are expected to be comprehensive, they must usually provide access to specialty services which will only be used by members with complex health problems. For example, only a very small proportion of health plan members will ever require the services of a endocrinologist or a heart transplant specialist. Because the use of these specialists is so unpredictable and small, it does not make sense to ask them to share in the risk of a managed care plan. However, the health plans try to control costs by entering into fee-for-service contracts with these types of providers at lower rates than the providers would usually charge.

Health plans may also help the providers in their network control costs through group purchasing of such things as medical supplies and pharmaceuticals with market share discounts. Another tool for controlling costs is for providers in a network to share services, such as administrative support for billing.

8. Quality assurance programs are required to assure that needed care is delivered in a timely way, that consumers are satisfied with the services, and that prevention measures are provided.

While sharing in risk may create incentives for doctors to keep patients healthier, the system is also structured so that doctors make more money in managed care if they deliver fewer services and make fewer referrals to specialists. Just as a fee-for-service approach creates opportunities for fraud and abuse through overtreatment, the managed care approach creates opportunities for fraud and abuse through undertreatment. In both cases, quality assurance programs are needed to assess whether the system is working to meet patients' needs. However, the focus of quality assurance and quality management is different in each system. In managed care, the focus of quality assurance and quality management is on delivering appropriate services in a timely and comprehensive way.

Case Studies as an Approach to Understanding Managed Care

Each of the four case studies selected for this project is intended to help illustrate how managed care works. Cases have been selected from different parts of the country and from different types of Indian health delivery systems within the I/T/U[1] spectrum. The case studies are a snapshot in time reflecting the systems as they were in 1996, recognizing that they have changed since then.

---

[1]"I/T/U" is the shorthand expression for the three types of health care within the Indian Health Service (IHS). These are the direct services provided by the IHS ("I"), the services delivered by Tribes through contracts or self-governance compacts under the Indian Self-Determination Act ("T"), and urban Indian programs ("U").

The first case study is Chief Andrew Isaac Health Center (CAIHC) in Fairbanks, Alaska. This case is intended to make people feel comfortable with the concepts of managed care because they are very similar to features that are already part of the delivery of Indian health services. Organized to follow the eight principles defined in the introduction, this case study illustrates the principles in practice. CAIHC is tribally operated by Tanana Chiefs Conference, Inc., under a self-governance compact.

The Pascua Yaqui Health Plan in Tucson, Arizona, is the second case study. This is the first and only time that the Indian Health Service has purchased a managed care plan with Contract Health Service dollars as an alternative to a direct care Service Unit. Started as an innovative program in 1980, the Pascua Yaqui Health Plan provides insights into how managed care contracts work. The relationships between the purchaser, the plan, the providers, and the consumers are defined in this case study. This case also illustrates how to create continuity of care for consumers as their eligibility for Medicaid managed care programs changes.

Third in these case studies is the Indian Health Board of Minneapolis in Minneapolis, Minnesota. This urban Indian clinic is a provider under contract with several Medicaid managed care plans. In this case study, the perspective of the provider is explored. As providers, urban Indian clinics face special challenges in accessing Medicaid funding in a managed care environment. Here, the provider is relatively powerless in negotiating rates, enrolling members, or absorbing the costs of serving Medicaid patients. Strategies for survival are limited for the small provider in the managed care environment, which favors large HMOs; however, the experiences of the Indian Health Board of Minneapolis offer insights for other providers.

The Mashantucket Pequot Tribal Nation in Connecticut is the subject of the fourth case study. Successful gaming operations have made the Pequot Tribe the largest employer in Connecticut, with over 12,000 employees. The Tribe owns, funds, and administers a managed care health plan that serves both employees and Tribal members. The Pequot Pharmaceutical Network (PRxN) is a tribally owned enterprise that makes money on managed care. In this case, the Tribe has taken advantage of the opportunities offered by managed care to define a health benefit package, to design a program that serves Tribal members and employees through the power of combined volume purchasing, and to develop businesses which serve other Tribes and organizations operating managed care health plans.

Each of the case studies describes how the systems are organized. This includes the roles and contractual relationships of purchasers, plan, and providers; how money flows through the system; and how consumers receive health care services. While the case studies are not intended as evaluations, there is recognition of what works well and some of the challenges that confront Indian health programs in managed care settings. People in leadership and management roles in managed care in these settings offer their advice to other Tribes.

The Future of Managed Care

Managed care is the wave of the future. Virtually everybody in the health care industry agrees that managed care will continue to grow, that both Medicaid and Medicare will enroll more people in managed care plans, that profit-making corporations will be the fastest growing segment of the managed care market, and that federal government regulation will increase for the managed care industry.

The terms used in this report, and defined in a glossary at the end, are considered the foundation from which managed care is evolving. Just as the entire managed care industry is changing, the Indian health programs in these case studies are changing. Survival and success of health care organizations depend upon their ability to monitor trends and adjust to the marketplace.

One of the major trends is the shift in responsibility from the federal government to state governments. When President Clinton's proposed health care reform failed to pass Congress in 1992, many of the ideas related to managed care continued to be implemented at the state level. For the most part, the federal government has not regulated managed care, leaving that role to states. While Tribal sovereignty has established a government-to-government relationship between Tribes and the federal government, the same type of relationship does not exist between Tribes and most states. In the managed care setting, the federal trust responsibility and protections are diminished. For both Medicaid and Medicare, as well as employer-purchased health benefits, Indian health programs are entering into contracts with private health plans.

As Tribes are taking more responsibility for managing their health care delivery systems, they have had to become knowledgeable about the whole federal system of funding and administering health programs, which is rapidly changing through new legislation and regulations. Now Tribes are also expected to become knowledgeable about managed care so that they can negotiate contracts with states, health plans and providers. These case studies are intended as a starting place from which to learn the basics about managed care in a context that is relevant to Indian health care.

Chapter 2

Case Study of
Chief Andrew Isaac Health Center

Athabascan People of Interior Alaska

The Athabascan people have lived in Interior Alaska and Canada for thousands of years. They speak a language that is similar to Navajo and Apache. Athabascans led a subsistence lifestyle moving in small bands to hunt and fish in the boreal forests. They had small settlements along the rivers which became villages of permanent residence after European contact. In 1867, the United States acquired Alaska from Russia through the Treaty of Cession. Language in this treaty entitled Alaska Native peoples to the same laws and regulations that the United States adopts with regard to other Native American peoples.

Tanana Chiefs Conference

In June of 1915, the leaders of the bands came together to meet with Judge Wickersham who was the territorial governor. This historic meeting was the beginning of the Tanana Chiefs Conference (TCC), which advocated on behalf of the Athabascan people in Interior Alaska in Native land claims and other issues. After passage of the Alaska Native Claims Settlement Act (ANCSA) in 1971, TCC became a nonprofit corporation providing health and social services to Alaska Native people in the 225,000 square-mile area of Interior Alaska. ANCSA recognized each predominately Native village in Alaska as a Tribe. Each of the 43 Tribes in Interior Alaska has a representative on the Board of Directors of TCC.

TCC is organized into six subregions. Four of the six subregions are served by the Interior Service Unit of the Indian Health Service (IHS), which also serves the Eskimo village of Anaktuvuk Pass and the Alaska Native people residing in the urban area of Fairbanks. Shortly after the Indian Self-Determination Act (P.L. 93-638) was signed into law in 1975, TCC contracted with the IHS to assume a number of services. Each Tribe had the option to give a resolution to TCC to contract on their behalf.

TCC began a tribal-specific health planning process in 1979 which led to major changes in the delivery of health services. As a result of the TCC study and recommenda-

Entrance to Chief Andrew Isaac Health Center.

tions, the IHS decided to close the Interior Service Unit hospital which was built in Tanana in 1941. The village of Tanana, which was once at the center of the region because it is located at the junction of two major rivers, was no longer well situated after airplane travel replaced river travel and Fairbanks had become the largest community in the region with more sophisticated medical care. Instead of using money for building a replacement hospital, federal funding was made available to build Chief Andrew Isaac Health Center (CAIHC) in Fairbanks as part of the new Fairbanks Memorial Hospital. Operational funds from the old hospital were put into the Contract Health Services budget to purchase services from the private sector in

Fairbanks and to develop subregional centers with midlevel practitioners. This plan was implemented in 1982. In 1984, TCC received a P.L. 93-638 contract to manage the Interior Service Unit and Chief Andrew Isaac Health Center.

TCC was a leader in urging all regional Native nonprofit health corporations in Alaska to form a single compact with the IHS. The compact was signed on October 1, 1994. Each of the cosigners has a separate annual funding agreement with the IHS. Approximately 92 percent of the Alaska Native population is included in this compact. Some Tribes chose not to give a resolution to their regional nonprofit corporation to compact on their behalf. The Alaska compact resulted in downsizing the Alaska Area Office of the IHS by 33 percent originally, with further reductions scheduled to 15 percent of the precompact size.

The compact was expected to bring an additional $25 million into tribal health programs in Alaska: about $10 million from the Area Office, $6 million from IHS Headquarters and $7 million from contract support. The full contract support funding has not yet materialized and the debate over whether Tribal shares are subject to contract support has been resolved by establishing an agreement that 80 percent of Tribal shares go into new programs that are eligible for contract support. The compact has resulted in an 11 to 12 percent increase in funding for regional Native nonprofit health corporations. In 1996, this meant that TCC received $1.6 million for Tribal shares. TCC has used half of the additional funding from compacting to meet needs identified by the Tribes, such as safe water projects, medical supplies and equipment, and training for village health workers.

Today TCC has approximately 400 employees and owns an office building in Fairbanks, a patient hostel, an adolescent substance abuse treatment center, three alcohol recovery camps, two subregional health centers, 30 village clinics, and assisted-living housing for the chronically mentally ill. In addition to CAIHC, TCC operates a dental clinic, an optometry clinic, an environmental health program, a mental health program, a village home health program, health education, and Women, Infants and Children (WIC) nutrition program. TCC also compacts with the Bureau of Indian Affairs (BIA) to provide such services as education and employment, realty, village public safety, social services, and tribal government services.

TCC faces many challenges in the delivery of health services. The 43 Tribes in the TCC region are small, ranging in size from about 50 to 300 people. Most villages are not on Alaska's very limited road system. Travel by airplanes for people and supplies is expensive. There is little employment in the villages, so people rely on seasonal jobs and subsistence activities. While TCC doctors and dentists travel to the villages once or twice a year, most of the day-to-day health care is provided by local residents who are trained as community health aides (CHAs). The CHAs are supervised by midlevel practitioners in the subregional centers. The CHAs have daily telephone consultations with the physicians at CAIHC. CAIHC pharmacists mail drugs to village patients and stock the village clinic with medicines. CAIHC also coordinates prenatal care, immunizations and care of high-risk patients in the villages.

While TCC is organized and designed to serve the Athabascan people living in the villages in Interior Alaska, about half the Alaska Native people in the TCC region live in Fairbanks. Among the Alaska Native population in Fairbanks, about half are Athabascan and half are Eskimo. CAIHC serves both village and urban people, both Athabascan and Eskimo. The direct health care at CAIHC is provided to all who are eligible for the IHS. Contract Health Services are limited to those IHS-eligible individuals who reside in the Interior Service Unit and do not have alternate resources.

Managed Care in Alaska

It is 1996. Managed care organizations have not yet reached Alaska. The population density is so low that in most communities there is no private sector health care. Except for Anchorage, no towns have more than one private hospital and it is a struggle to recruit and retain physicians. The private sector is organized into individual practices and group practices which have no incentive to become health

Chief Andrew Isaac Health Center waiting room and appointment desk.

maintenance organizations (HMOs). In Fairbanks, the private physicians are just beginning to organize an independent practice organization (IPO), which will probably include everyone who wants to participate, and the school district has just issued a request for proposals for a primary care gatekeeping function. Most people in the health care industry in Fairbanks believe that managed care is still two to three years away.

Chief Andrew Isaac Health Center

In this most unlikely place, we can find many of the principles and best practices of managed care flourishing at the tribally operated Chief Andrew Isaac Health Center (CAIHC). Operated by Tanana Chiefs Conference, Inc. (TCC), CAIHC serves approximately 12,000 people, including 6,000 Alaska Native people residing in Fairbanks and another 6,000 living in 37 small isolated villages throughout the Interior Service Unit. CAIHC provides about 70,000 outpatient visits a year in a new 28,500 square foot clinic with a staff of 96 full-time and part-time people, including seven physicians, eight mid-level practitioners, and seven pharmacists.

In FY 96, the cost of direct services was $6.5 million, while the Contract Health Services spent approximately $7 million to purchase services from the private sector, including $550,000 for transportation. CHS pays for about 600 hospital admissions per year (including about 20 percent of the 255 deliveries to CAIHC patients), and 6,800 emergency room visits. In addition to IHS funding, CAIHC generates billings of approximately $1.8 million, including $1.4 million in Medicaid reimbursements, $397,000 in private insurance collections, and $28,000 in commissioned officer health care reimbursements.

Managed Care Principles in Action

This case study is organized around the principles outlined in "What is Managed Care?" in the introduction to this book. CAIHC activities are used to illustrate the principles of managed care in an Indian health setting.

1. A health plan defines benefits and limitations for the consumer at a fixed annual cost.

There are two aspects to this principle: a benefit package and a fixed annual cost.

The CAIHC benefit package is not listed in one place, such as one would expect to find in a contract between a health plan and its consumers and/or purchasers. Nevertheless, the benefits are defined. The scope of health services provided directly by the clinic is defined in the *Patient Handbook*, policies and procedures, and the Quality Management Plan. Policies and procedures define how services are provided through Contract Health Services and which services are excluded. For some types of services, such as bone marrow transplants, patients are referred to the IHS tertiary care system where the concept of a defined benefit package has not been developed.

The main source of funding for CAIHC is the IHS. Traditionally, the IHS received its funding from Congress and then apportioned it to Area Offices which in turn apportions it to Service Units. With compacting, this process has been altered slightly, but the same results occur: There is a fixed annual budget from the IHS. This concept of a fixed annual budget, or a "global budget," means that organizations must operate within a set budget regardless of the demand for services. CAIHC does supplement its IHS budget by billing insurance companies and Medicaid for patients who have these alternate resources.

2. Health care providers are part of networks organized by health plans and defined by contractual relationships.

CAIHC is connected to several different formal networks, including Tanana Chiefs Conference (TCC), the Indian Health Service (IHS), and the Alaska Federal Health Care Partnership. Additionally, the Contract Health Services (CHS) program within CAIHC has developed a network of contractual relationships with private sector medical providers.

Physicians and other health care providers at CAIHC are expected to practice according to the privileges they have been granted, the policies and procedures, and the protocols and guidelines developed by the clinic. They are generally limited to prescribing from the formulary in the pharmacy at CAIHC, which is decided by a committee of clinicians, pharmacists and administrators who consider both effectiveness and cost. They are limited in how and to whom they can refer patients. And they operate within a network of programs and providers at CAIHC who share responsibility for managing patient care.

Within the TCC organization, there is a network of providers at the village, subregional and regional levels. These are interrelated by supervisory relationships and referral practices. Physicians at CAIHC supervise midlevel practitioners in the subregional centers, who in turn supervise community health aides (CHAs) in the villages. Physicians at CAIHC also provide direct medical consultation to

CHAs. Patients in the villages flow through a referral system from the CHA to the midlevel practitioners in subregional centers to the physicians at CAIHC.

CAIHC is also part of the IHS network. Physicians at CAIHC may refer patients to the Alaska Native Medical Center (ANMC) in Anchorage, which is the statewide referral and tertiary care center for the Alaska Area of the Indian Health Service. Physicians at ANMC in turn refer patients to other parts of the IHS network, including the centers of excellence under contract with the IHS. CAIHC uses the IHS Resource and Patient Management System (RPMS), training programs, and the central warehouse in the Area Office. Also, CAIHC employs a number of Commissioned Corps physicians, pharmacists, and nurses through Intergovernmental Personnel Act agreements. Historically, the Area Office provided quality and management oversight of programs, but that function generally has been eliminated with compacting. The relationship between CAIHC and the IHS is defined in compacting agreements between TCC and IHS.

In 1995, federal agencies providing health services in Alaska joined together in the Alaska Federal Health Care Partnership. Participating agencies included the IHS, Veteran Affairs, the Army, the Air Force, and the Coast Guard. Recognizing that the Tri-Care initiative in the Department of Defense would not work in Alaska because there are no managed care plans with which to contract, the federal agencies developed their own approach to reducing costs through group purchasing, joint contracting and sharing services. CAIHC was able to participate in the Alaska Federal Health Care Partnership because several military health care facilities are located in the Fairbanks area, including Bassett Army Hospital (BAH). A Memorandum of Agreement was signed between TCC and the U.S. Army Medical Department Activity–Alaska which defines the relationship.

Since 1979 when TCC became involved in planning for the future of the Interior Service Unit of IHS, there has been a growing relationship between Indian health care and the private medical providers in Fairbanks. There is close interdependence between CAIHC and Fairbanks Memorial Hospital, a facility built by the community and operated under contract with Lutheran Hospitals and Homes. After occupying a 10,450 square-foot clinic within the hospital for many years, CAIHC moved into 28,500 square feet of newly remodeled space in Fairbanks Memorial Hospital on April 1, 1995. The hospital financed the construction and remodeling for the $5.2 million project. TCC will pay back $4.5 million of the costs at 6 percent interest through a 20-year lease. IHS provided $300,000 to equip CAIHC from a $3-million fund for new tribally owned clinics.

CAIHC has enjoyed a 24-year history of colocation with the community hospital, that has provided the advantages of easy access to sophisticated laboratory and radiology services; convenience for doctors in admitting patients; ability to transfer patients to and from the emergency room; efficiency for doctors, community health nurses and Contract Health Services personnel in making rounds on inpatients and coordinating with hospital staff; and access for staff to the cafeteria and meeting rooms. With an average daily census of 16.36 Alaska Native patients (including newborns and those with alternate resources), it is not feasible for Tanana Chiefs Conference to operate its own hospital. However, by combining patients and resources with the Fairbanks community hospital, Alaska Native people in Interior Alaska enjoy specialty medical services and a high standard of care. Contracts with FMH not only provide for leasing space, but also for maintenance, housekeeping, sterilization, laundry, and other services to CAIHC. FMH provides hospital services at a 15 percent discount through its contract with CAIHC.

Contract Health Services (CHS) at CAIHC also has negotiated contracts with medical specialists and group practices in the Fairbanks area to provide specialty medical care. These contracts define credentials, malpractice insurance requirements, referral practices, and payment rates. Patients who are served by private physicians through CHS generally have their prescriptions filled at the CAIHC pharmacy where the pharmacists enlist the cooperation of the private doctors in prescribing items in the formulary. Since there is

Contract Health Services office.

only one OB/GYN working for CAIHC, that physician shares
call with OB/GYNs from a private group practice. Relationships between CAIHC and medical specialists in the private
sector are further defined by the fact that all have privileges at
Fairbanks Memorial Hospital, which sets community standards for credentialling, malpractice insurance, and practice
guidelines.

Using the analogy of managed care, TCC generally fills
the role of the health plan with IHS purchasing the plan for
IHS beneficiaries. TCC in turn provides primary care services directly and contracts with Fairbanks Memorial Hospital and private physicians to provide specialty medical care.
TCC uses the IHS network to provide additional care.

3. Primary care providers are generally paid a fixed amount for each patient assigned to their care.

IHS provides a fixed amount to TCC to deliver health services to all eligible people within the Interior Service Unit. TCC in turn gives a portion of that money to CAIHC to provide primary care and to manage the Contract Health Services program. CAIHC operates within a fixed budget and serves a defined population. While a capitation rate, or average cost per person, could be calculated, the budget numbers are not strictly based on population.

IHS funding formulas have developed over time based upon a variety of factors, including both population size and a geographic factor, which takes into account the variations in cost of providing services. When the Alaska compact was designed, the Tribes decided not to redistribute any recurring base funding. However, they used a formula for the distribution of Tribal shares, which is 35 percent based on user populations.

Throughout the country, user populations have grown within some Tribes as a result of higher birth rates, lower death rates, higher percentage of tribal members using services due to changes in employment and insurance, and higher tribal enrollments as a result of changes in eligibility criteria. While IHS has recognized the need to increase budgets to respond to population growth, Congress has not provided sufficient funding to keep pace with this trend. As a result, the overall funding of IHS is not directly linked to the number of people served. Neither is it responsive to the number of services provided. Because the money is allocated as a lump sum at the beginning of the year and because the original formulas were developed with population as a factor, it is more similar to capitation than fee-for-service.

It should be noted that CAIHC does receive compensation on a fee-for-service basis from those patients who have private insurance. CAIHC is also reimbursed for services to patients who have Medicaid coverage. In Alaska, the Medicaid reimbursements for IHS and tribal facilities are neither fee-for-service nor capitated. Medicaid pays a flat rate per day for any and all services provided. In 1996 in Alaska, the outpatient rate was $233 per visit day. This is paid by Medicaid whether a patient receives an ear re-check or they have a colonoscopy or both. The Medicaid rate was determined using a formula based on Medicare rates with additional cost adjustments.

4. Financial risk is shared by the providers.

Because the IHS budget is a fixed amount, TCC must provide all the services at CAIHC within the amount budgeted (plus insurance and Medicaid reimbursements). If the money runs out before the end of the fiscal year, TCC must absorb the costs of care until new money is available for the next fiscal year. It should be noted that TCC is a nonprofit corporation and that there is no gaming in Alaska, so this tribal organization does not have the option that many other Tribes around the country have of drawing on resources from tribal economic development to supplement health revenues.

Before TCC took over management of the Interior Service Unit, there were times when the money for Contract Health Services ran out before the end of the fiscal year. When that happened, patients would have to wait until new money came in the next fiscal year to receive contracted services, or vendors would have to wait until the next fiscal year to be paid. One benefit that was realized when TCC became a contractor under P.L. 93-638 was that money left in the budget at the end of the fiscal year could be carried forward into the next fiscal year. This carry-forward, which could last three years, allowed TCC to accumulate a reserve (unlike the federal government which operates on a "use-it-or-lose-it" policy).[2] This reserve creates a cushion against unanticipated expenditures.

The concept of assuming risk means that TCC is responsible for providing health services to all of its constituents all year long within the available budget. Since most of the patients do not have insurance or Medicaid, this means that spending more on health care does not mean increasing income. TCC is a consumer-owned nonprofit corporation. The people who receive services are also the owners of the corporation. The consumers elect the Board of

---

[2]More recently, amendments P.L. 93-638 and the revised regulations allow Tribes to carry over funding without time limits and to earn interest on these funds.

Directors. This creates a great incentive for the Board of Directors to manage the funds wisely and in the best interest of all consumers.

The TCC Health Board and Board of Directors have chosen to exclude or limit spending for certain types of services (such as infertility treatments) so that there will be more funds available for basic services. The Boards have placed an emphasis on providing preventive services to reduce the costs of health care. And the Boards have directed management to implement policies and procedures that conserve expenditures so that there will be sufficient funding to meet the needs of everyone without running out of funding at the end of the year. For the past decade, these practices, along with the aggressive billing of third parties and the development of a computer system to manage CHS expenditures, have resulted in a stable, consistent delivery of services.

5. Total risk is limited through reinsurance or stop-loss plans.

The budget for primary care, or direct services, at CAIHC is fixed and services are provided within the budget. This is fairly predictable, and there is little risk to the organization.

Specialty medical services and inpatient care are paid through the Contract Health Services (CHS) program. The budget for this program is approximately $7 million. This covers the ordinary costs of serving the population. However, a single car crash with an uninsured driver can result in medical bills exceeding $150,000. A complicated gunshot wound can require multiple surgeries and months of rehabilitation. An organ transplant can consume an inordinate amount of money.

The risk of incurring the costs of these very expensive and unpredictable medical conditions is managed through two mechanisms. The first is the Catastrophic Health Emergency Fund (CHEF) within the IHS, which is available to all IHS-funded CHS programs. CHEF is the IHS self-insurance stop-loss plan. It is a reserve account which can be used after the CHS program meets a minimum payment for a single episode of care. The threshold for CHEF is $17,700 in 1996. If medical bills for a single patient for a single episode of care exceed this amount, CAIHC can request reimbursement from CHEF for amounts over this threshold. CHEF generally reimburses CAIHC between 50 and 80 percent of the amount over $17,700. The reason that the amount of reimbursement varies is that the CHEF is a reserve of $12 million, and claims often exceed this amount in any given year. In addition to the IHS Headquarters CHEF reserve, the Alaska Area Office keeps a reserve of $1.2 million to help pay for unfunded CHEF claims.

The second way that CAIHC limits its risk of absorbing large medical costs is to use the Alaska Native Medical Center (ANMC) and its referral system. ANMC is the only medical facility in Alaska directly operated by the IHS, and its budget covers the cost of care delivered there. It is the tertiary care referral center for all Service Units in Alaska. ANMC also operates a CHS program for patients whose medical needs require specialty care not available at ANMC. Once a patient is referred to ANMC, the costs of referrals outside the IHS system or outside the state of Alaska are absorbed by the ANMC budget. Compared to the other Service Units, the Interior Service Unit underutilizes ANMC because the resources are generally available to serve patients in the Fairbanks area, while most other Service Units are in remote areas that lack private sector specialty care.

ANMC provides a sort of "safety valve" for the CHS program at CAIHC. Here is how it works. CHS funding for the year is budgeted by month. The CHS program and the medical staff set a threshold for nonemergency procedures (such as hernia repairs, biopsies and other diagnostic procedures). Recently this threshold has been $1,500 for professional charges. If a nonemergency specialty medical need costs less than $1,500, then the CAIHC physicians refer the patient to a physician in the Fairbanks area through the CHS program. If the cost is estimated to be more than $1,500, then the patient is referred to ANMC. If the CHS budget is being spent too quickly, then the threshold can be set lower, at $1,000 for example. If CHS funding exceeds expenditures, then the threshold can be set higher. For patients with insurance, Medicare or Medicaid, only the amount of the deductible which would be paid by CHS is used in the calculations. There is a strong patient preference to stay in Fairbanks to receive care, and this is balanced with the management goal of staying within budget and not running out of funding before the end of the fiscal year.

A by-product of the ANMC referral alternative is that private physicians in the Fairbanks area often adjust their prices to keep patients. For example, at a recent time when the threshold went down to $1,000, the physician's charge to CHS for cataract surgery in Fairbanks fell to $999.

Both CHEF and ANMC limit the financial risks to CAIHC. They allow CAIHC to provide its benefits package to consumers without exceeding a fixed global budget. They do this by covering the cost of care which exceeds a predetermined threshold.

6. Case management, preadmission screening, utilization review, formularies and copayments are used to provide services in the most economical way.

CAIHC uses case management, preadmission screening, utilization review, and formularies to provide services in the most economical way. Unlike most managed care systems, copayments are not used by CAIHC because IHS beneficiaries are entitled to free health care.

Case management at CAIHC is provided by a Community Health Nursing staff, as well as primary care providers. Each has a distinctive role.

The primary care providers and midlevel practitioners serve as gatekeepers to specialty care. Before CHS will authorize a visit to a specialty medical provider in the private sector, the primary care providers at CHS must make a determination of medical necessity and weigh the costs and benefits of using CHS versus referring the patient to ANMC. This is usually done by the primary care providers in the context of a patient visit. However, there are times when patients have already been referred to a private physician and that physician wants authorization to provide additional services or recommends referring the patient to another private provider. On a daily basis, the medical director or another designated physician at CAIHC reviews these requests and decides whether to recommend CHS funding or an ANMC referral or to bring the patient back to the medical services at CAIHC.

Patients with high-risk or special needs are assigned to case managers in the Community Health Nursing program at CAIHC. Case management is provided on an ongoing basis for patients with the following diagnoses: diabetes, cancer and other terminal illnesses, HIV positive and/or AIDS, arthritis with methoirexate medication, and high cholesterol with high risk. Care coordination is provided during the specific period of need for all patients in the following categories: pregnant women, women with abnormal Pap smears, women with abnormal mammograms, village elders who require hospitalization, and children with special needs. In addition, the chronically mentally ill receive case management services from the TCC mental health program.

Within Community Health Nursing, there are several programs which provide focused case management services. Two of these programs, the Elders Program and the Pap Program, are highlighted here to illustrate the scope of services provided under case management.

The Elders Program has three nurses who provide care coordination to approximately 560 people, including 160 with diabetes, 212 with cancer, and 150 who are chronically ill and over 18 years old. They also serve about 1,000 people over 60 years old who do not have chronic disease, but do have episodic needs such as fractured hips, cataracts, or the need for placement in long-term care. Referrals to the Elders Program come from physicians, family members and other agencies in the community. The nurses in the Elders Program provide health surveillance on elders, including chart reviews on village elders before a physician visits the village to identify the current health surveillance measures needed according to established protocols, letters to elders reminding them that they are due for appointments, patient education, followup after a doctor visit to assure that lab tests which were ordered were done, appointment coordination, and making transportation arrangements for village elders (including meals and lodging, if needed). The nurses make home visits and assessments, make agency referrals and followup, and participate in discharge planning. They also try to educate people about how to use the health care system, and assist people in making living wills, advance directives, and durable powers of attorney. Additionally, the Community Health Nursing Program established a cancer support group to meet the needs of patients and family members. Case management also includes working with the CHS Alternate Resource Specialists in identifying and helping elders to get the paperwork completed to qualify for alternate resources such as Social Security, Disability, Medicare, Medicaid, Veterans Affairs, CHAMPUS, and other military benefits. The role of these nurses is to assure that everything is done to keep the patients healthy and to reduce complications and hospitalizations.

Another effective case management program at CAIHC is the Pap Program, which is managed by one nurse using a register, a tickler file, and the computerized RPMS provided by IHS. This nurse tracks every Pap smear that is done at CAIHC. She receives results daily via computer and contacts patients who have abnormal results to return for a repeat test. If the repeat test is also abnormal, she schedules patients for a colposcopy which is offered three days per week at CAIHC. With two treatment rooms and two practitioners providing colposcopies, approximately 15–20 procedures are provided each week, allowing for quick followup. The Pap nurse receives the biopsy reports and notifies the patients of results. Using standing orders, the Pap nurse then arranges the followup, which could be antibiotics, cryotherapy, laser treatment, or a leep procedure. All of these are provided in-house at CAIHC. If patients do not show for any of their appointments, the Pap nurse calls them and reschedules their appointments. Because early diagnosis and treatment is provided, the number of cases of invasive carcinoma has been reduced dramatically. When invasive carcinoma is diagnosed, the Pap nurse makes arrangements to refer the patient to an oncologist/gynecologist at ANMC.

In addition to case management, the Community Health Nursing staff provides other services that target prevention. An immunization coordinator uses RPMS and coordinates with community health aides, state public health nurses and subregional centers to assure that people receive their immunizations on a timely basis. As a result, 90 percent of village children under 2 years old and 88 percent of Fairbanks children in this age group have received all recommended immunizations. Another example is the patient educator on the Community Health Nursing staff, who provides patient education and counseling for people with diabetes, people seeking HIV testing, and those interested in weight loss, smoking cessation and other lifestyle changes. A nutritionist is also available for counseling and to assist with the WIC program. In addition to the patient educator at CAIHC, TCC employs a staff of five health and safety educators who travel to the villages to increase community awareness about injury prevention and health promotion, including such goals as wearing life jackets and installing smoke detectors.

Since TCC took over management of the Interior Service Unit, one of the fastest growing areas has been Community Health Nursing, which now has a staff of 21 plus 43 people who have been trained as certified nursing assistants to serve as personal care attendants to people in the villages needing home health services. The growth in Community Health Nursing reflects an emphasis on quality assurance, quality management, prevention, early diagnosis, and care coordination. All of these activities are designed to improve health status and patient satisfaction. At the same time, they serve to reduce duplication of services and limit more expensive care from complications and hospitalization.

Reducing the costs of hospitalization also is accomplished by preadmission screening and utilization review. Prior to or during hospitalization, the CHS alternate resource specialists review each person's eligibility for alternate resources, such as insurance, Medicaid, Medicare, Veterans Administration, and military benefits. They assist people with the paperwork necessary to obtain the resources for which they may be eligible. Fairbanks Memorial Hospital (FMH) understands that CHS is the payer of last resort and cooperates in billing other resources first. Patients without alternate resources who are expected to have lengthy or costly hospitalizations may be sent to ANMC for the initial hospitalization or transferred there when they are stable.

Each day a member of the CHS staff and the medical director or another designated physician reviews the list of inpatients at FMH and their current and expected length of stay in an attempt to make timely decisions about step-down care at the less expensive adjacent skilled nursing facility or other discharge plans. The expectation is that patients will not stay in the hospital more than four days. In the past, there were times that patients stayed an extra day in the hospital just because their doctor didn't get around to discharging them, but this no longer happens with the more proactive approach to utilization review. The average length of stay for patients whose bill is paid by CHS is 3.6 days, compared to 4.11 for Native Americans with alternate resources.

The CAIHC pharmacy has a formulary which is reviewed and revised by a Pharmacy and Therapeutics Committee that includes pharmacists, physicians, midlevel practitioners, and administrators. The committee considers all of the drugs available in a given category and compares their costs and benefits. Pharmacists who research these options provide a service to the physicians who may not otherwise know the comparative costs of drug options. An agreement to include a drug in the formulary means that health care providers will generally prescribe that drug when needed. Costs are reduced because the inventory in the pharmacy is reduced. Also, the pharmacy purchases most drugs off the federal schedule, which results in savings as a result of the volume of federal purchasing. Finally, there is a commitment from everyone involved to use the least expensive choice among drugs that are the same chemically.

7. Costs are controlled through a variety of measures, such as discounts in contracts with providers and group purchasing through networks.

Traditionally, the Indian Health Service has used group purchasing, often in combination with the Veterans Administration, to obtain pharmaceuticals and nursing supplies at costs well below market wholesale prices. The IHS Alaska Area operates a warehouse where CAIHC can order these items. Monthly shipments are made from the warehouse in Anchorage via truck to Fairbanks. Items which are not in stock at the time of the monthly shipment are sent later via air mail.

In the 1996, CAIHC discovered it could reduce the cost of supplies by using the Alaska Federal Health Care Partnership prime vendor contract, which offers prices below the IHS warehouse for most items. The prime vendor makes daily shipments to Bassett Army Hospital (BAH) in Fairbanks with a 24-hour turnaround time for orders. CAIHC developed an agreement with BAH to stock the nursing supplies at CAIHC. A limited number of supplies are kept on rolling carts with computerized bar codes in a storeroom at CAIHC. Twice a week, a person from BAH brings a full cart and takes the cart from which supplies have been used to BAH to fill it and replace outdated supplies. This arrangement has reduced the space needed for storing supplies and has relieved the nursing staff from the tasks of ordering, inventory, and unpacking supplies. Most important, it has resulted in a 70 percent savings in cost of supplies! The cost of nursing supplies has gone from about $200,000 per year to about $60,000 per year. Using the same system, CAIHC has reduced the cost of office supplies from about $50,000 per year to $12,000 per year.

CAIHC has been very effective in negotiating contracts with private sector providers. This is particularly true for Fairbanks Memorial Hospital (FMH), which provides services at 85 percent of its published rates. This is the largest discount that they give and compares favorably to the Preferred Provider discount of 2 percent that they give to Blue Cross. CHS payments represent only about 5 to 7 percent of FMH revenues. When the new clinic was remodeled, FMH included a satellite laboratory and X-ray facility at CAIHC so that patients would not have to walk to another part of the hospital to receive these services. Still, CAIHC recognized that it could save money by sending laboratory tests to a larger reference laboratory. CAIHC was able to negotiate a significant reduction in prices from FHM. Laboratory expenses dropped from approximately $500,000 in FY '93 to $187,000 in FY '95.

CHS has also negotiated favorable contracts with private physicians and physician groups in the Fairbanks area. Many of the private physicians like to see Alaska Native patients because they present different medical challenges than they see with their usual patients. Also, some of the private physicians previously served in the IHS and want to maintain their ties to the Native communities. The physicians at CAIHC maintain generally good relationships with private sector physicians, enhanced through participation in hospital committees and the local medical society. CAIHC physicians tend to refer to the private physicians with whom they have the best communications and who understand the peculiarities of the IHS system. Cost is less of a factor in selecting medical specialists than good working relationships. Nevertheless, CHS asks for and often receives discounts.

In 1995, the Alaska Federal Health Care Partnership issued a request for proposals for physician care. They awarded a contract to a private group practice clinic in Fairbanks, which offered an immediate 25 percent discount in rates with further discounts based on volume. This discount was below the CAIHC discount of 20 percent, so CAIHC was able to take advantage of the Alaska Federal Health Care Partnership rates. The contract did not prevent CAIHC from referring to private physicians outside the group. Physicians at CAIHC report that their referral patterns did not change, but they did save money by participating in this network contracting.

8. Quality assurance programs are required to assure that needed care is delivered in a timely way, that consumers are satisfied with the services, and that prevention measures are provided.

CAIHC is accredited by the Joint Commission on Accreditation of Healthcare Organizations (JCAHO), receiving accreditation with commendation on the past two surveys. Quality assurance and quality management are an integral part of the accreditation requirements. CAIHC has a nurse designated as quality management and infection control coordinator, but virtually all staff participate in quality management activities ranging from committee meetings to studies. Consumer satisfaction is measured by surveys and investigation and followup on all patient complaints. Systems are in place to provide, track, and measure prevention activities, including immunizations, Pap smears, mammograms and well-child visits.

A built-in quality management system is that pharmacists review charts prior to filling prescriptions to assure that the diagnosis is appropriate for the medication and that health surveillance measures needed for certain medications are done in a timely way. Case management activities of Community Health Nursing staff are another way to assure that protocols and guidelines for the management of chronic diseases are followed and that needed care is delivered in a timely way. Another aspect of quality management is continuing education for clinic staff. In FY '95, CAIHC spent approximately $30,000 on training and continuing education for staff in all departments, with additional training provided by IHS, TCC, and the State of Alaska, at no cost to CAIHC.

Challenges for the Future

While CAIHC has achieved considerable success in the delivery of health services, management and staff have identified areas for improvement. Some of the challenges identified include increasing the number of tribal members in leadership, management, and professional positions. Only two of seven key management positions at CAIHC are filled by tribal members.

Traditional healing is a service that consumers want at CAIHC, and the Tribes support this goal. While a limited amount of traditional healing is practiced at CAIHC and within the region, it is an area in need of further definition, discussion, and direction.

In an organization as large as TCC, there is a continual challenge to make sure that communications are effective at all levels and in all places. There is a tension between the needs perceived in the villages and the plans designed at the regional offices. In the demand for more local control, there is often a lack of understanding of the economies of scale (that larger organizations may be less costly than smaller ones) and that it is difficult to recruit, retain, and supervise health professionals in small, isolated communities. Health care in the Alaska Native communities is not just about the delivery of quality services, but also about employment, economic development, local control and tribal sovereignty.

What Works Well

Chief Andrew Isaac Health Center did not set out to be a managed care organization. The history of affiliation with the Indian Health Service and the desire to deliver high-quality services has led CAIHC to implement practices which are consistent with principles of managed care. There are several reasons that managed care principles work well in this setting, and these are likely replicated in other settings:

1. CAIHC has a demonstrated commitment to excellence.
2. Tanana Chiefs Conference, Inc., (TCC) has a long history of health care management beginning in 1973 and progressively has taken more responsibility for programs, including contracting under P.L. 93-638 in 1976 and compacting in 1994. Generally, TCC has been conservative about financial management, building a reputation for fiscal responsibility and maintaining a reserve rather than spending all income.
3. TCC has consistently placed an emphasis on prevention programs and on delivering services as close to the place where people reside as possible. These two

values have resulted in the development of a health care delivery system which is well integrated, responsive to local needs, and evolving steadily in the same direction.

4. Local control and effective fiscal management means that TCC has been able to operate with priorities that reflect the needs and the preferences of the people served. For example, all cancer treatment is provided in Fairbanks when the services are available there, because the people do not want cancer patients to have to leave the support of their family and community, and they trust the medical care they receive from the local oncologist. TCC provides services not usually funded by IHS, such as transportation for patients from the villages to Fairbanks and return (CHS spent approximately $550,000 on patient transportation in FY '96).

5. Health care providers at CAIHC are team players. Doctors welcome case management of patients by nurses and chart reviews by pharmacists. Everyone participates in decision making that balances costs with needs for patient care. Shared responsibility for developing the formulary and the rules which govern Contract Health Services referrals lead to shared responsibility for carrying out those decisions.

6. People in key positions have had experiences outside the Indian Health Service (I/T/U) system, which

make them aware of different ways of approaching problem solving. The Director of Contract Health Services, for example, brings several types of skills to his job which make him able to balance patient needs with financial resources. His experience and credentials include being a registered nurse, earning a Master's in Public Health, experience in financial management including being licensed as a securities broker and an insurance agent, and computer skills.

7. Several people in key leadership positions at CAIHC, including the Health Center Director and the Director of Contract Health Services, are retired from the military. The comfort level with the military, their networks, and their ease of communications helped to facilitate CAIHC participation in the Alaska Federal Health Care Partnership.

8. There have been long-term, stable relationships between CAIHC, FMH, and the private sector. The interrelationships make each considerate of the needs of the others. Negotiations are generally friendly and mutually beneficial. Financing from FMH provided a new clinic for CAIHC when no federal funding was available.

Chapter 3

Case Study
of the Pascua Yaqui Health Plan

History of the Pascua Yaqui Tribe

Pascua Yaqui Indians descended from the ancient Toltecs in the Yaqui River Valley in the area that is now Sonora, Mexico. While Yaqui territory spread northward into what is now Arizona, it was not a part of the United States until 1854. European contact began in 1533 with Spanish exploration. In 1617, Jesuit missionaries introduced the Catholic religion, and within two years 30,000 Yaquis were baptized. Spain established a fort in Tucson in 1776 and ruled the area until Mexican independence in 1821. In 1846, the United States went to war with Mexico and acquired most of the land north of the Gila River in the treaty of 1848. The Gasden Purchase in 1854 added land south of the Gila River to the United States. The purchase of this land by the United States resulted in the loss of land ownership by the Yaquis. By the time the Arizona Territory was established in 1863, most of the Yaquis consolidated into communities south of the border.

In the 1800s, the Mexican government began a policy of genocide against the Yaquis. In 1868, Mexican troops killed 450 Yaquis by burning them in a church. Later, the Mexican government sent thousands of Yaquis to Yucatan as slaves. The Yaqui people say that as late as 1929, the Mexican government had a bounty on Yaquis. To escape persecution and extermination, Yaquis fled to the Arizona Territory. Between 1880 and the granting of statehood to Arizona in 1912, several Yaqui communities were established near Tucson and Phoenix. By 1920, there were an estimated 2,000 Yaquis in Arizona.

In 1964, Congress transferred 202 acres of desert land southwest of Tucson to the Pascua Yaqui Association, a nonprofit corporation formed to receive the land. At the same time, the Administration for Native Americans started providing annual funding of approximately $100,000 per year to the Pascua Yaqui Association. The land grant became the basis for a reservation, to which an additional 690 acres were added in 1982. Today, the Pascua Yaqui Reservation has a total of 970 acres. In 1978, Congress recognized the Pascua Yaqui Tribe, giving it a unique status as a "created" Tribe which had more limited benefits than "historic" Tribes. Tribal enrollment began in 1978 and extended for three years. Enrollment was low because people did not fully understand the benefits of tribal enrollment and some were afraid that tribal enrollment would lead to further persecution. At the end of the enrollment period, there were about 3,000 enrolled tribal members. Only those who enrolled prior to 1981 and their descendants could be considered tribal members. In 1988 a constitution was approved and a council was elected.

The Pascua Yaqui Tribe was the second Tribe in the nation, and the first in Arizona, to have Indian gaming. A bingo hall was established in 1982. Today, the gaming operation has about 500 employees of whom 95 percent are Tribal members. Gaming proceeds are being used to supplement federal budgets and to build infrastructure on the reservation, including a new health clinic. Tribal employment, including tribal administration, gaming and other tribally owned industries, has been responsible for reducing the unemployment rate from an estimated 78 percent in 1980 to 23 percent in 1993.

In 1994, Congress changed the Pascua Yaqui Tribe's status from "created" to "historical" Tribe. The legislation (P.L. 102-357) also reopened enrollment for three years and called for a study to determine whether funding formulas for the Pascua Yaqui should be readjusted by the Indian Health Service and the Bureau of Indian Affairs. The Secretary of Interior was to submit a report to Congress in October 1996 with recommendations. Tribal officials predicted that the new enrollment period would result in a total of approximately 12,000 to 15,000 members.

Yaqui culture and ceremonies incorporate both the Catholic liturgy and traditional tribal customs and beliefs, including the belief in other worlds, the power of nature, and the deer dancer. The word "Pascua" refers to Easter, which is the most important ceremonial event for the Pascua Yaqui people. Most Pascua Yaqui tribal members are bilingual, speaking both English and Spanish. The Yaqui language is still spoken by tribal elders and a revival of the language is occurring among the youth. There is ongoing communications between the Pascua Yaqui people in Arizona and the Rio Yaqui people in Sonora, Mexico.

Healing traditions have survived in the Pascua Yaqui community. There are different types of Yaqui healers, including those who practice massage, herbalists, and midwives. Today, massage is used most frequently. It is also called "touch healing" or "nerve healing." Spiritual traditions are also considered part of the healing process.

Most Pascua Yaqui live in seven communities in two counties in Arizona. Three of these communities are in Maricopa County, which surrounds Phoenix: Guadalupe in Tempe, Penjamo Pueblo in Scottsdale, and High Town Community in Chandler. In addition to the Pascua Yaqui Reservation, there are three other communities in Pima County: Old Pascua in Tucson, Barrio Libre in South Tucson, and Yoem Pueblo in Marana.

Rebecca Tapia and Rebecca Martinez at the ceremonial grounds and community center of Old Pascua.

Innovation Within the Indian Health Service

The Pascua Yaqui Health Plan is unique for several reasons. Within the Indian Health Service, it is the only Service Unit that is totally contracted with a managed care plan. Pascua Yaqui Health Plan members can move between the Tribal health plan and the Arizona Medicaid managed care program with complete continuity of care. With a capitation rate of $77.53 per member per month in 1996, the cost of care is below market costs for health care in the Tucson area. An explanation of how this is done may provide insight for other Indian health programs.

When the Pascua Yaqui Tribe was recognized in 1978, it was anticipated that tribal members would be provided health care through the Indian Health Service (IHS) system. The Pascua Yaqui Reservation lies within the IHS Tucson Area, which was created in 1967 to serve as both an Area Office and as the national research and training center for the IHS.

The IHS faced some limitations in serving the Yaquis in existing facilities. In the Tucson Area, the two facilities operated by the IHS were the outpatient clinic at San Xavier, where the IHS Area Offices were located near Tucson, and the hospital at Sells, about an hour drive from Tucson on the Tohono O'odham Reservation. The San Xavier clinic was overcrowded and the Sells hospital was too far away. The waiting list for new IHS facilities was already lengthy, and it would be a long time before federal dollars would be available to build a clinic on the Pascua Yaqui reservation. With only 3,000 Tribal members, many of them living outside the Tucson area, it would be difficult to justify building and staffing a new hospital and/or clinic.

The trend in the IHS was to purchase specialty medical services from the private sector through Contract Health Services (CHS) funding, a line item in the federal budget which is separate from hospitals and clinics funding used to operate IHS facilities. In keeping with this trend, it was decided to use CHS funding to provide services to the Pascua Yaqui tribal members in the Tucson area. Tribal members in the Phoenix area could have access to the Phoenix Indian Medical Center

(PIMC), which served as both an urban Indian clinic and a referral hospital for the IHS in the Phoenix Area.

Private sector health care in Arizona had developed managed care plans earlier than most of the rest of the country. When the IHS conducted a feasibility study of interest in the local medical community, managed care was one approach considered. The advantage of this approach was that there would be a fixed, predictable budget. Furthermore, the managed care plan would not require the administrative costs and staffing to authorize and process bills in a fee-for-service approach. In the IHS bureaucracy, the Service Unit level of organization was eliminated and the contract was managed by a single individual in the Area Office. Since there had never been a Pascua Yaqui Service Unit, this approach did not meet opposition which would likely be expected from employees if a Service Unit were proposed for elimination. However, it should be noted that the Pascua Yaqui tribe accepted the plan under protest in 1980, preferring to have the more traditional bricks-and-mortar approach to providing health care within the IHS.

El Rio Health Center became licensed as an HMO in 1980 and was the first contractor under the Pascua Yaqui Health Plan. El Rio's rapid expansion led to a financial crisis, including a large debt to Carondolet Health Care, which owns and operates St. Mary's Hospital and St. Joseph's Hospital in Tucson. Carondolet helped El Rio resolve the problem by creating the Southwest Catholic Health Net-

El Rio Health Center main offices in Tuscon, Arizona.

work, which is 51 percent owned by Carondolet and 49 percent owned by St. Joseph's Health Care Center in Phoenix, which in turn is owned by Catholic Health Care West in California. The newly created Southwest Catholic Health Network took over El Rio's Pascua Yaqui contract and made El Rio a subcontractor for ambulatory care.

Today, Southwest Catholic Health Network has offices in Phoenix and manages contracts under the Arizona Medicaid managed care program in three counties (Pima, Maricopa, and Santa Cruz), Developmental Disabilities contracts in nine counties and a managed care plan for businesses with fewer than 40 employees. At one time, Southwest Catholic had 80,000 members enrolled in its plans,

St. Mary's Hospital, operated by Carondolet, serves members of the Pascua Yaqui Health Plan and Mercy Care.

but with the entry of Blue Cross and CIGNA into the market, the Southwest Catholic enrollment dropped to about 60,000 members. The Pascua Yaqui Health Plan represents less than six percent of its enrollment.

Providing and Managing Patient Health Care

As people are enrolled in the Pascua Yaqui Health Plan, they are asked to select a primary care provider (PCP) at the El Rio Health Center or its satellite clinic on Valencia

Appointment desk for new pediatric clinic at El Rio Health Center.

Road. For adults, the PCP can be either an internist or a family practice physician. For children, the PCP can be either a family practice physician or a pediatrician. Approximately 80 percent of Pascua Yaqui Health Plan members select primary care providers at the main clinic and 20 percent use the satellite clinic. The patient's medical records are kept at the clinic where the primary care provider is based. Many of the primary care providers have office hours in a small clinic on the Pascua Yaqui reservation on a rotating basis. When they are working on the reservation, they bring the medical records for patients with appointments with them.

Patients must make appointments with their primary care provider. A limited number of appointment spaces are reserved for walk-in or urgent-care needs, but these are usually filled by telephone by 8:00 a.m.

Primary care providers make referrals to specialists and order other health services both within the El Rio Health Center and affiliated with other health care organizations, including St. Mary's Hospital and St. Joseph's Hospital. The Pascua Yaqui Health Plan will not pay for specialty medical services unless they have been authorized by a primary care provider affiliated with the El Rio Health Center. Specialty care available at El Rio includes internal medicine, pediatrics, and obstetrics-gynecology. Pregnant women without complications may choose to be served by nurse midwives. El Rio obstetricians also provide prenatal care and attend deliveries at St. Mary's Hospital. High-risk deliveries are done at St. Joseph's Hospital or the Tucson Medical Center.

Patients may have prescriptions filled either at El Rio Health Center or two private pharmacies which are open 24 hours per day. While El Rio has a formulary which limits medications provided to most patients, if a doctor prescribes medicine not on the formulary, the Pascua Yaqui Health Plan generally pays. Patients may receive dental care either at El Rio or from two other contracted dentists.

Members of the Pascua Yaqui Health Plan who experience problems in health care services or have questions about alternate resources may contact a patient advocate. There are two patient advocates, one located at El Rio

Health Center and one at the Office of Health Planning on the reservation, both funded by IHS.

The Tribe provides transportation services to and from health care. There is a tribally operated van that picks up people at designated bus stops on a regular schedule and delivers them to the El Rio Health Center. People can call a day ahead to reserve transportation to other places for appointments.

Financial Structure and Risk in the Health Care Delivery System

The Tucson Area IHS contracts with Southwest Catholic Health Network. This contract includes a capitated portion which is paid per patient per month and a fee-for-service portion. All of the official reporting and invoicing goes from Southwest Catholic Health Network to IHS. All of the financial payments go from IHS to Southwest Catholic.

Southwest Catholic Health Network subcontracts with El Rio Health Center and St. Mary's. The capitation rate part of the contract is divided between El Rio Health Center and St. Mary's Hospital, with Southwest Catholic Health Network keeping a reserve amount for administration, self-insurance and to cover deficits at the end of the contract year.

The subcontract with El Rio is capitated, which means that they receive a fixed amount per patient per month.

This amount is divided into two accounts. One is used for El Rio's direct operations and the other is used to subcontract with medical specialists who are not employees of El Rio Health Center. El Rio Health Center assumes full risk for ambulatory care, medical specialty care, and pharmacy. This means that El Rio must absorb any costs that exceed the amount paid in the capitated rate.

The Southwest Catholic Health Network, subcontracts with St. Mary's Hospital providing a fixed amount per patient per month; however, there is no risk to St. Mary's. The subcontract essentially provides a pool of funds on which to draw on a fee-for-service basis. At the end of the contract year, if St. Mary's costs exceed the monthly payments, an adjustment is made from the reserve account retained by Southwest Catholic Health Network. It should be noted that Southwest Catholic Health Network also contracts with St. Joseph's Hospital and the Tucson Medical Center for inpatient care.

Southwest Catholic assumes risk up to $50,000 for a single patient's hospitalization. IHS provides reinsurance for members whose inpatient care exceeds $50,000. This has only been used once in the past 6 years, possibly because the Arizona Medicaid program has a medically needy provision which covers most cases which would otherwise fall into this category.

Under the fee-for-service portion of the IHS contract, Southwest Catholic Health Network manages several programs for IHS with no risk. When the amount of money allocated for these services, such as hearing and vision, is fully expended, the service simply is not provided to additional patients until additional funds are made available. The contract between IHS and Southwest Catholic Health Network also contains fixed amounts to pay for a patient advocate and for meeting the reporting requirements.

One expectation of managed care is that services are prepaid at the beginning of the month. However, government financial procedures result in payments retrospectively rather than in prospective payments. Sometimes it takes as long as 90 days for IHS to pay its monthly bill from Southwest Catholic Health Network. Because the contract is relatively small and Southwest Catholic has sufficient cash reserves to continue its operations, this has not been perceived as a problem.

Role of the Pascua Yaqui Tribe

Tribal participation is addressed in the contract between IHS and Southwest Catholic Health Network with this wording:

The Contractor shall be responsible for ensuring that maximum Tribal participation shall occur as demonstrated through Tribal Representation in a Governing or similar Board or committee regarding this contract. Policy and decision changes which may or will affect the Yaqui patients or Pascua Yaqui Health Department shall be discussed with both the IHS and Pascua Yaqui Tribe a minimum of ten (10) days prior to implementation. Prior to discussion, the Contractor must submit in writing to the IHS and the Pascua Yaqui Tribe a description of desired changes as a written notice. The IHS reserves the right to deny the Contractor the policy change until all three parties are in agreement with the requested change.

Beyond these and a few other contract provisions, the role of the Pascua Yaqui Tribe in the managed care plan has not been well defined. There is no Memorandum of Agreement between IHS and the Tribe outlining roles and responsibilities. Until 1994, the Tribe was not involved in reviewing the Request for Proposals (RFP) or selecting a contractor. Since then, the Tribe has been privy to financial information and involved in the negotiations.

The requirement in the contract for the Contractor to consult with the Tribe at least 10 days before implementing new policies has been carried out in the spirit of full consultation often taking months to explore the potential effect of decisions. The only option presented to the Tribe for greater involvement in contract management is to take over the entire contracting process through a P.L. 93-638 contract with the IHS. Because the Tribe was newly created and inexperienced in managing health care, this responsibility seemed too risky at first. However, the Tribe has

received several planning grants which have enabled their
Office of Health Planning to acquire the personnel, expertise and experience to undertake management of the contract. It was anticipated that the Tribe would assume contract management in 1997. It is generally believed that
Tribal management of the contract will be less bureaucratic
and less restrictive in contracting procedures than the federal government and will be able to be more innovative in
negotiating better deals.

Since 1981, the Tribe has provided some health services
under a P.L. 93-638 contract with the IHS. These include
community health nursing, community health representatives, medical social work, transportation, special programs
for diabetes and HIV/AIDS, mental health, alcohol and
substance abuse prevention, rehabilitation counselors and
treatment homes (funded under the BIA contract). Because
the Tribal health programs are serving the same people who
are receiving services at El Rio Health Center, either through
Medicaid or the Pascua Yaqui Health Plan, there is a need
for communications and referrals. Referral requirements are
explicitly recognized in the Pascua Yaqui Health Plan
contract.

Most of the tribal health programs have been funded at
less than optimal levels. While the Tribe is essentially providing home health services, it is not licensed as a home
health agency and cannot collect reimbursement from Medicare, Medicaid, or other third parties. One goal of the Tribe

is to become a licensed home health agency and then to sub-contract with El Rio Health Center to provide home health care.

Representatives of the Pascua Yaqui Office of Health Planning, including the Director, the Quality Assurance/ Utilization Review (QA/UR) nurse, and the patient advocate attend the monthly contract meetings. Both the patient advocate and the QA/UR nurse also attend the weekly discharge planning meetings. Other tribal health staff also attend the weekly discharge planning meetings, including the community health nursing supervisor, the community health representatives supervisor, the long-term planning coordinator, the alcohol and substance abuse coordinator, and the medical social worker. Discharge planning meetings provide an opportunity to share information and coordinate care for patients more broadly than just those being discharged from the hospital.

Through the patient advocate and the informal communications network, the Tribe is active in trying to solve problems which patients encounter. Tribal employees have open communications with management of the Southwest Catholic Health Network, El Rio Health Center, and IHS. While the tribal role may be unofficial, it is powerful. The players understand that the Tribe will be managing the contract eventually, and they want to please the Tribe.

The Tribe has a contract with IHS to enter data received on reports from Southwest Catholic Health Network into the IHS Resources and Patient Management System (RPMS). While RPMS was designed to help manage patient care in an IHS setting, the information from the Pascua Yaqui Health Plan is not used for patient care.

In addition to the management role, the Tribe has a political role. New enrollment in the Tribe creates the need for additional funding. The Tribe can advocate for congressional appropriations to meet this need. In the absence of new funding, the Tribe must work within the Tucson Area Office of IHS to assure that formulas used to distribute appropriations are fair and responsive to the needs.

"Seamless" Movement of Tribal Members Between the Pascua Yaqui Plan and the State Medicaid Managed Care System

When the Pascua Yaqui Health Care Plan was established in 1980, the state of Arizona did not have a Medicaid program. Indigent care was provided through a system of county hospitals as Arizona was the last state in the country to accept federal dollars through Medicaid. The Arizona Health Care Cost Containment System (AHCCCS) includes both the Medicaid program, which receives a 65.85 percent federal match, and indigent health care funded entirely with state and county dollars for those who do not qualify for Medicaid. It was started as a managed care program in 1982 under a Section 1115 Research and Demonstration Waiver from the Health Care Financing Administration (HCFA). AHCCCS began as a system for primary, preventive and acute medical care. Later, other components were added, including the Arizona Long Term Care System (ALTCS) in 1988 and behavioral health services in 1990.

AHCCCS provides health care through 14 contracted health plans. Each offers a prepaid, capitated approach with the health plan assuming risk for the delivery of services to enrolled members. As of 1994, every county in Arizona offered AHCCCS recipients a choice of at least two health plans. In Pima County, where Tucson and the Pascua Yaqui Reservation are located, there are six AHCCCS plans.

Because the Pascua Yaqui Health Plan was in place prior to AHCCCS, the state and IHS worked together to design elements which would promote continuity of care as tribal members became qualified or disqualified for AHCCCS.

One of the AHCCCS plans is Mercy Care which is operated by Southwest Catholic Health Network. The Pascua Yaqui Health Plan is also operated by Southwest Catholic Health Network. In Pima County, both plans use the El Rio Health Center for ambulatory care and St. Mary's and St. Joseph's Hospitals for inpatient and emergency care. While Pascua Yaqui tribal members who qualify for AHCCCS are offered the Mercy Care plan, they are not required to take this plan. However, they are allowed to switch to the Mercy Care plan without the customary wait (6-month lock-in period) which is required of other AHCCCS recipients. And Pascua Yaqui members who qualify for AHCCCS and do not choose a plan are given the Mercy Care plan as a default assignment.

Both Mercy Care and the Pascua Yaqui Health Plan require members to select a primary care provider who becomes the gatekeeper to specialty services. Yaqui patients can keep the same primary care provider regardless of whether their monthly premium is being paid by AHCCCS or by the IHS. This means that the health care for Pascua Yaqui tribal members continues uninterrupted with the same providers even though they change plans. When they change plans, the only thing that changes is that the bills are paid from a different source of funding.

Because the Pascua Yaqui Health Care Plan is funded from IHS Contract Health Services, there is a requirement that alternate resources be used first. The plan contains a provision for on-site screening for alternate resources. AHCCCS enrollment can begin within three days after eligibility is established and extends for six months, so there is a continuous flow of patients on and off the system. After much negotiation and technical work, it is possible to use the computer to identify Yaqui members of the AHCCCS plan and assure that the proper organization is billed.

A unique aspect of this managed care arrangement is that the provider actually generates the lists of members for the Pascua Yaqui Health Plan each month.

It should be noted that AHCCCS does not pay for medications, but the IHS contract covers this for AHCCCS patients who would otherwise be enrolled in the Pascua Yaqui Health Plan.

Low Cost of Care From Nonprofit Providers

When the Pascua Yaqui Health Plan was started in 1980, the capitation rate was $47 per patient per month, including outpatient care, inpatient care, and dental. The contract has been rebid every three years, with the highest rate being $79 per patient per month. The 1996 capitation rate was $77.53. However, this rate excludes dental, physical therapy, ambulances, alcohol and substance abuse treatment, and mental health. Some of these items, which were in previous contracts, were pulled out and contracted separately due to low utilization rates.

The average number of monthly enrollees is 3,526 for an annual capitated contract value of $3,280,449.36. Other services are included in the contract on a fee-for-service basis, such as home health, physical therapy, medical social services, nutrition consultation, and a patient advocate. In FY '96 the Tucson Area Office had one-time funding to add vision and hearing to the benefit package. These are handled on a fee-for-service basis with a limited amount allocated for the services. This brings the total annual amount to $3,438,524.76, which averages to $975 per person per year, an equivalent of $81.25 per person per month.

The IHS Area Office pays for ambulances, dental and chemical dependency treatment through additional Contract Health Services funding which is managed by the Pascua Yaqui Tribe Office of Health Programs. The IHS Area Office provides mental health services directly. And through P.L. 93-638 contracts, the Tribe provides community health services, such as public health nursing, community health aides, and health education programs.

It is estimated that the cost of the Pascua Yaqui Health Plan is 20 percent below the cost of similar benefit plans in the private sector. It is less than the AHCCCS capitation rates, which vary from a low of $93.99 per patient per month for women eligible for Medicaid under the SOBRA option to a high of $312.77 per patient per month for persons eligible for Medicaid under SSI without Medicare. The AHCCCS rates are set by the State of Arizona using an independent actuarial firm to develop rate ranges. For the Pascua Yaqui Health Plan, the IHS issues a RFP to all licensed managed care plans in Arizona, including all AHCCCS plans, with no limitations on costs in the RFP. As of 1996, only El Rio Health Center and Southwest Catholic Health Network have ever bid on the Pascua Yaqui Health Plan.

As the number of AHCCCS plans increases in Arizona and the enrollment in the Pascua Yaqui Health Plan grows, it might be anticipated that other companies would offer proposals. However, there are several factors which may discourage other organizations from bidding on the plan. These include the perception that Native Americans generally have poor health and are expensive to serve, the elaborate and unconventional reporting requirements that IHS has written into its contracts, high startup costs with a steep learning curve for a new contractor, the higher administrative costs for coordination with IHS and tribal representatives, and the historical relationship between the current providers and the Pascua Yaqui Tribe.

Even before federal recognition and the IHS payment for Pascua Yaqui health services, the Pascua Yaqui people received their health care from El Rio Health Center and St. Mary's Hospital. Both providers are nonprofit corporations formed to serve the needy. St. Mary's Hospital was started by seven of the Sisters of St. Joseph of Carondolet who made a dramatic 36-day journey from St. Louis via San Francisco to Tucson in 1870. The hospital was built in 1880 and has been expanded many times since then. It is owned by the Tucson-based Carondolet Health Care, which also owns St. Joseph's Hospital in Tucson and Holy Cross Hospital in Nogales, as well as other health care facilities and programs.

El Rio Health Center started in 1970 with a grant from the University of Arizona. When that funding ended in 1974, a community board was formed, and the clinic became a community health center with federal funding. In 1977, a new clinic was constructed nearby the Old Pascua community in downtown Tucson. The Angel Charity for Children raised $700,000 to build a pediatric center on the campus of the El Rio Health Center in 1992. The pediatric building also houses dental and optometry services, as well as health education classrooms. A satellite clinic was constructed in southwest Tucson on Valencia Road near the Pascua Yaqui Reservation in 1995. Since 1986, El Rio Health Center also has rented space from the Tribe to provide limited clinical services on the reservation.

El Rio Health Center receives three federal grants to underwrite its service as a community health center, to provide health care to the homeless, and to serve HIV/AIDS patients. Also, the local United Way provides a pharmacy fund that purchases medication for patients who cannot afford it on a one-time basis. Approximately 50,000 people are served by El Rio Health Center. About 10 percent of these are Pascua Yaqui Health Plan members, 30 percent are AHCCCS recipients enrolled in any of the six plans offered in Pima County (including Mercy Care), 35 percent are self-pay patients who receive health care on a fee-for-service basis with a sliding scale based on ability to pay, and the remaining 25 percent have other third-party coverage. Approximately 75 percent of the patients are ethnic or racial minorities, and 85 percent are low income.

All of the parties involved in the Pascua Yaqui Health Plan—Southwest Catholic Health Network, El Rio Health Center, and Carondolet operating through St. Mary's and

St. Joseph's hospitals—have a mission of service. They all express a willingness to serve the Native American population on a break-even basis. They understand the need to provide a culturally sensitive environment and take actions not required in their contract to be responsive. For example, when a patient requests a traditional healer, St. Mary's Hospital cooperates to enable the traditional healer to practice in the hospital. El Rio Health Center actively recruits bilingual and Pascua Yaqui staff members. Approximately 13 percent of the 300 employees are Native American, a higher proportion than the patients served. The former medical director of El Rio Health Center is an enrolled member of the Pascua Yaqui Tribe and currently serves on the Tribe's Health Planning Advisory Committee.

For the providers, the principle of service seems to be a stronger guide to decision making than the contract. The contract is fairly vague about the benefit package, but there is virtually no bickering between parties regarding what is covered and what is not. Patient needs seem to take a higher priority than cost containment. Leadership in each of the organizations is involved on a personal level to assure that the Pascua Yaqui Health Plan is implemented with flexibility and cooperation above and beyond the requirements of the contract. The providers define themselves as carrying out a mission rather than being part of a bureaucracy.

People involved in the management of the contract from both IHS and the Tribe have been former employees of El

Rio Health Center and/or Southwest Catholic Health Network. They understand how these organizations operate, have access to the highest levels of leadership and enjoy excellent communications. There is a high degree of appreciation and trust between all parties.

Limitations and Challenges

Because the Pascua Yaqui Health Plan is funded through Contract Health Services (CHS), eligibility is more restrictive than if health care were provided directly by the IHS or by the Tribe under a self-determination (P.L. 93-638) contract or compact. CHS eligibility rules include not only tribal membership, but also residency within a CHS service area. Only Pascua Yaqui Tribal members who reside in Pima County (the Contract Health Services Delivery Area) are eligible to enroll in the Pascua Yaqui Health Plan. Those who reside in Maricopa County and elsewhere do not have this option and cannot access IHS services.

Another limitation is the inability of the budget to meet the needs of increased membership. When the Pascua Yaqui Health Plan was started, the annual cost was approximately $500,000. Now the cost exceeds $3.4 million. Because the Indian Health Service is not considered an entitlement program and the current climate in Congress is to cut federal budgets, there is no assurance that appropriations to the IHS will increase in response to population increases. As the number of members enrolled in the Pascua Yaqui Health Plan increases, the cost goes up proportionately. Unlike the IHS direct services which absorb these increases with an attitude of "doing more with less," the capitation approach requires that services be eliminated from future contracts to serve more people with the same amount of money.

Greater coordination between tribal employee benefits packages and the Pascua Yaqui Health Plan could increase the resources available for health care. Present policies encourage tribal employees to reject the employee health plan and to enroll in the Pascua Yaqui Health Plan. While the employee health plan gives people an option to use El Rio Health Center, they must pay deductibles and copays which are not required under the Pascua Yaqui Health Plan.

If Pascua Yaqui Health Plan members have a complaint, it is that they have a difficult time making appointments. Even though the health plan requires a maximum waiting time of 14 days for appointments, patients say that they sometimes wait as long as six weeks. Patients who cannot get appointments for urgent care often are referred to the emergency room at St. Mary's Hospital. Patients also complain that once they arrive for their appointments, they often have long waits in the waiting room and the exam rooms. Some patients say that it is easier to get appointments to see their primary care providers at the reservation clinic; however, laboratory facilities are minimal there, so there are limitations in medical care. Patients say they would

Jack Rameriz, Planning Director, Pasqua Yaqui Tribe with plans for the new clinic on the reservation.

like to have more time to talk with their providers. They feel that providers are often overworked and rushed, so they frequently only treat the chief complaint and do not address other complaints.

People residing on the Pascua Yaqui Reservation would like more clinical services available on the reservation, including laboratory, X-ray equipment, and more physicians. The Tribe committed gaming revenues to construct a new 4,660 square foot clinic which will be leased to El Rio Health Center to provide services under the Pascua Yaqui Health Plan. Construction was expected to be completed by the end of 1996. The new clinic will also house a dialysis center and have a courtyard for traditional healing ceremonies. Both Health Department and Health Planning Department employees will be located in the same place. A Tribe which does not have gaming revenues may be less able to address the need for a facility on the reservation.

The managed care contract offered by IHS has not kept pace with changes in the industry. Specifically, there is minimal quality assurance reporting required, and the only quality standard in the contract is a maximum 14-day wait for appointments. Waiting times for appointments, in the waiting rooms, and in the exam rooms could be reduced as the single most important factor in improving patient satisfaction. Also, the contract contains reporting requirements to meet IHS standards that are not found in most managed care contracts. For example, the providers must report all diagnoses of sexually transmitted diseases to IHS, a requirement that would be considered a violation of privacy with regard to any other purchaser of services. Many of the reporting requirements cannot be met through existing computer-billing systems, so they require time-consuming manual systems. The contract has some other unusual conditions, such as El Rio Health Center buying supplies for the Public Health Nurses employed by the Tribe.

Advantages of the Pascua Yaqui Plan

There are many advantages to the Pascua Yaqui Health Plan. There is a defined benefit package, and tribal members do not worry about services being diminished at the end of the fiscal year due to depletion of Contract Health Services funding. By contracting with nonprofit organizations, the cost of care is low. The quality of health care and the kinds of services provided are considered good. Continuity of care is maintained as patients move between the Pascua Yaqui Health Plan and the AHCCCS plan.

There were no startup costs or capital costs to begin the delivery of health services to this newly recognized Tribe. While the location of services is generally regarded as convenient, people want to be served close to home and look forward to expanded services on the reservation when the new clinic is built. El Rio Health Center provides employment and management internship opportunities to Pascua Yaqui tribal members.

A guiding principle of managed care is that a regular source of health care can reduce hospital inpatient utilization by as much as 66 percent. This is particularly true for diseases like diabetes and high blood pressure, which are especially prevalent among Native American populations in the Southwest. Managed care also provides an opportunity to focus on early detection and prevention of diseases. El Rio Health Center reports that breast cancer screening is higher among those enrolled in the Pascua Yaqui Health Plan than among the general insured population.

Since the Pascua Yaqui Health Plan was implemented successfully in 1980, it has never been duplicated within the IHS. Some people believe that the conditions for this innovation have not been present in other settings. These conditions include: 1) a small, newly recognized Tribe with no accessible, existing IHS facilities to serve them; 2) close proximity to an urban area with a private health care delivery system; 3) a tradition of managed care within the private sector; 4) the availability of a nonprofit health care system, which will serve the Indian community at relatively low cost; and 5) an IHS Area Office willing to seek innovative solutions.

Advice for Others Considering a Managed Care Plan Like Pascua Yaqui

The following advice was offered and reiterated by people in management from the Pascua Yaqui Tribe, the IHS, Southwest Catholic Health Network and El Rio Health Center:

1. The managed care plan and providers should be considered a partner in a long-term relationship. It is important to find a good partner, one who shares your philosophy and beliefs, who has experience dealing with similar populations, and who is culturally sensitive. It takes at least three years to identify and resolve problems. Organizations should not be judged on their initial performance, but rather their efforts

to make improvements to get things to run smoothly. For this reason, the first contract should be at least a three-year contract.

2. Involve the Tribe in every step of the process from the beginning.

3. Pay attention to things beyond finance. The Tribe or IHS should not just be a purchaser of health care, they must become a part of the system. This means that management should attend meetings, work to solve problems, and advocate for patient needs.

4. Don't contract with the lowest bidder on the basis of cost alone.

5. The contract should specify expectations about quality management, utilization management, and long-term community health objectives.

6. Tribal members need to be educated about how managed care works and how to use the system effectively.

7. Staff who are hired to manage the contract, either through IHS or the Tribe, should have experience with private sector managed care plans.

8. Regular meetings between the contractor, the provider, and the Tribe are very helpful. In addition to weekly patient care coordination meetings (discharge planning meetings) and monthly contract management meetings, there should be regular meetings to make decisions about the formulary.

Chapter 4
Case Study of the Indian Health Board of Minneapolis

A History of Leadership in Urban Indian Health Care

The Indian Health Board (IHB) of Minneapolis is located in the Phillips Neighborhood in Hennepin County. The neighborhood is characterized by older two-story frame houses, some with windows boarded-up and others with fresh coats of paint. Within blocks of the IHB are several large hospitals, including Hennepin County Medical Center, Children's Hospital, and Abbot-Northwestern. Another hospital which closed was converted into Four Winds School, a magnet school serving Indian children. The people in this neighborhood are generally young, recent arrivals to the city and transient. American Indians comprise about a quarter of the Phillips Neighborhood population and most come to the city from Minnesota Tribes and bordering states.

In 1971, IHB was incorporated and became the first urban Indian health clinic in the country. The 11-member Board of Directors is 51 percent consumers and 51 percent American Indian. It has a proud history of national leadership in community health. In 1978, IHB was the first urban Indian clinic to receive funding from the U.S. Public Health Service "330" Urban Health Initiative. In 1985, IHB began participating in managed care through the Minnesota Medicaid 1115 Waiver Demonstration Project for Hennepin County. In 1986, IHB was the first urban Indian clinic and the first Minnesota Community Health Center to receive three-year accreditation from the Joint Commission on Accreditation of Healthcare Organizations (JCAHO). In 1990, IHB was the first community health center in Minnesota to be designated a Federally Qualified Health Center (FQHC). IHB was a leader in the formation of the Minnesota Primary Care Association and the association of urban Indian clinics called the American Indian Health Care Association (AIHCA).

The IHB serves people who are without resources, including battered women who have left their spouses, people who are chemically dependent, people who do not comprehend the state and county social service system and do not submit the paperwork to qualify for assistance, people who don't pay their bills and are not welcome in other settings, refugees, and undocumented aliens. Over 40 percent of the patients are children under 15 years old. Over 75 percent of the people served are American Indians.

The Indian Health Board of Minneapolis is a two-story structure above a parking area.

The IHB provides medical, dental, mental health, outreach and transportation services. IHB receives grant and contractual funding from the State of Minnesota and the Indian Health Service for specific programs, including the Women, Infants and Children's (WIC) nutrition program, immunizations, family planning, diabetes, and alcohol and substance abuse services. IHB provides case management for about 40 AIDS patients and an HIV prevention program. IHB averages about 34,000 patient encounters per year. Also, IHB provides about 10,000 rides, with four people operating five vehicles.

The clinic is staffed with 70 employees. There is no problem with recruitment and retention, except among the en-

try-level clerical positions. Most of the staff have long ten-
ure and know the patients well. One doctor has been with
the clinic since its inception. Most of the physicians are
women. The clinic staff is able to relate to their consumers
in a supportive manner because they truly respect the people
they serve and they have the patience to deal with people
who are in chaos and angry.

In the 1995 fiscal year, the total revenues for IHB were
$4.2 million of which 35 percent came from patient fees.
Only 10 percent of the IHB patients have private or employer-purchased health insurance. Among those who seek
care at the IHB, 42 percent do not have any payment source
and most of that care is uncompensated. Medicaid, or the
state Medical Assistance (MA) and GA (General Assistance), pays for 45 percent of the patients who receive care
at IHB. People over 65 years old comprise 2 percent of the
patients and Medicare pays for about 3 percent of the patients. Because so much of the care is uncompensated, the
IHB relies on 22 different grants and contracts. Including
income from billing, approximately 37 percent of the clinic's
support comes from the Indian Health Service, 10 percent
from the U.S. Public Health Service Urban Health Initiative and Perinatal Care Program, 8 percent from Hennepin
County, and 5 percent from the State of Minnesota Department of Health and Human Services.

IHB does more than provide health care. It also serves
as a cultural center for the Indian community. Feasts are

offered free to community residents for holidays and other occasions. Lunches are provided weekly for diabetics and pregnant women. The clinic hosts craft sales by local Indian artists. Not only does the clinic hold community meetings, but it is also a meeting place for representatives of Minnesota Tribes. Other community services include spiritual meetings, a seniors program, job training, women's support groups, and an education parent committee. In 1988, traditional healing was added to the scope of services at the clinic.

After serving the Indian population in the Phillips Neighborhood for 25 years, in 1995 the IHB decided to change its mission. Anticipating the declining revenues under Medicaid managed care, the elimination of Federally Qualified Health Center (FQHC) full cost funding, and a reduction in federal funding sources, the Board of Directors could only foresee that the Indian clinic would either change its focus to become a neighborhood clinic or become absorbed by another larger entity. The Board began to envision a new direction, which is based more on traditional Indian healing practices and serves a larger community.

Minnesota and Managed Care

In 1985, Minnesota applied for and received its first 1115 waiver for a demonstration project that would enroll a portion of Medicaid recipients in managed care plans. This demonstration was conducted in four counties. One of those counties was Hennepin County, in which Minneapolis is located. From the beginning of this demonstration project, the Indian Health Board (IHB) of Minneapolis became involved as a provider of health care under the state's Prepaid Medical Assistance Program (PMAP).

Minnesota provides coverage for health care services for more than 750,000 low-income, uninsured and individuals with special needs through Medical Assistance (MA), General Assistance Medical Care (GAMC or GA), and Minnesota Care Programs.

The MA program is essentially the Medicaid-funded programs covering acute, chronic and long-term health care for 430,000 state residents. Included with the MA program is PMAP, which serves 160,000 MA recipients, predominantly those who qualified for Aid for Families with Dependent Children (AFDC), which was later replaced by Temporary Assistance to Needy Families (TANF). The GAMC program, which has been in place since 1973, provides state-funded acute health care for approximately 47,000 residents who do not qualify for MA categorical assistance programs, but who do meet the asset and income requirements comparable to Medicaid's medically needy standards. Minnesota Care provides acute health care services for approximately 93,000 uninsured, with recipients paying for a portion of their care.

While Minnesota's first 1115 waiver only provided a demonstration project in four counties and for a limited number of consumers, a second 1115 waiver in 1987 expanded and continued the program. In 1994, Minnesota applied for a "cosmic waiver" which integrated MA, GA and Minnesota Care into a single Prepaid Medical Assistance Plan.[3] This 1115 waiver was approved by HCFA in April 1995 and changed the way health care was delivered statewide.

As with most states involved in managed care, Minnesota regards managed care as a form of purchasing health services on behalf of citizens who qualify for state-funded services. The state contracts with health plans on a capitated basis. There are different capitation rates for different groups of citizens, based on actuarial studies that predict the average costs per patient per month. The health plans are paid the capitated rate each month and they assume the risk for providing all the services required in their contract. The health plans then contract with doctors and hospitals and other providers to deliver the services. The contracts between health plans and providers can either be capitated or

---

[3] Some MA and GA patients are not enrolled in managed care plans. The principal is that the state cannot give a "burning house" to an HMO. The state pays for these individuals on a fee-for-service basis. IHB calls these patient "straight MA" and they constitute about $30,000 per month in revenues.

fee-for-service. Not all providers are required to assume risk. Those who assume risk are paid more than those who do not assume risk.

The State of Minnesota regulates managed care with a somewhat unique approach. First, the state requires that all health maintenance organizations (HMOs) and other types of managed care health plans be nonprofit organizations. Their financial status is open to the public. The state examines their books to know how much they spend in administrative costs (in 1996 it was 9 to 11.5 percent) and how much income they receive in excess of expenses. The state believes that it is reducing the cost of health care for everyone by requiring health plans to be nonprofits, because profit-making organizations would be expected to make a 12–15 percent return on investments.

Minnesota statutes and "Rule 101" make all health plans operating in the state participate in public programs. All health plans must accept up to 20 percent of their membership from state provided coverage. The health plans must accept these members at rates set by the state in order to do any other business in the state. Not only does the state "strong arm" the plans into participating in public programs, but the state also creates a powerful incentive for providers to accept PMAP patients. According to Minnesota statutes and regulations, any providers who accept any patients who are public employees must also see up to 20 percent of their patient base in PMAP clients. The state only requires that health plans pay providers at least as much as they would have been paid under the state fee-for-service Medicaid schedule.

The State of Minnesota tries to control the cost of health care by rate-setting methods that are approved annually by the state legislature. The capitation rate for 1996 is based on information collected in 1991, 1992, and 1993 and adjusted for changes in services. While the state believes that it is only requiring a 10 percent discount for the nonelderly and a 5 percent discount for the elderly, some of the plans maintain that the state capitation rate pays only 54 percent of their costs. The fee-for-service rate list used by the state in 1996 is based on usual and customary charges at the 50th percentile in 1992. The 50th percentile means that this is less than what half the doctors and hospitals were charging. Because the state fee-for-service rate list does not keep up with inflation, it is generally accepted that the fees are about 48 percent of standard charges.

The strategy that the State of Minnesota is using is to require health plans and providers to absorb the PMAP patients at a lower rate of pay than they would receive for their commercial accounts. This strategy requires there to be fewer and larger plans, so that the PMAP patients remain a minority, and the unpaid costs of their care can be shifted to other paying patients. Over the years, plans have consolidated and changed so that there are fewer and larger players. Statewide, there are nine plans in Minnesota. Five plans are operating in Hennepin County, and the Indian Health Board of Minneapolis contracts as a provider with four of those plans.

Health Plans in Hennepin County

The Medicaid health plans in Hennepin County represent a range of approaches for organizing payment and delivery systems. Medica, UCare and Metropolitan Health Plan are three of the plans that illustrate this diversity.

Medica is an "open access model" which means that patients can get their care anywhere in the network. Medica is provided by Allina, a company with a 100-year history and more than a million members. It offers a commercial product called, "Select Care," as well as "Medica," in 64 counties in Minnesota, Wisconsin, and North Dakota. Allina owns five hospitals in Minnesota and serves about one-third of the state's total population. While Medica covers 70,000 people in Minnesota, this is less than 10 percent of Allina's total business. Medica providers in Minnesota include the Indian Health Board of Minneapolis, as well as three tribally operated clinics. They do not have assigned primary care providers. Allina sees itself as a third-party administrator for the state, more like conventional insurance than managed care. While Allina is paid by the state on a capitated basis, all of their contracts with providers are on a no-risk, fee-for-service basis. Allina requires providers who contract under Select Care to also contract at a lower rate for Medica. Allina's parent company is United Health Care, one of the largest profit-making companies in the health care industry nationwide, with over $2 billion dollars in business annually.

UCare Minnesota is a plan developed so that the hospitals and doctors at the University of Minnesota could receive compensation from the state PMAP. Until recently, it was a "closed staff model," and there was no opportunity for clinics not affiliated with the university to become providers under the plan. However, the University hospital was purchased by Fairview Hospital, and the policy changed. It has had to expand the number of "feeder clinics" to provide patients in order to stay competitive. It is anticipated that there will be another takeover of the University Hospitals by Health Partners, one of the largest HMO's in the state.

Metropolitan Health Plan (MHP) is operated by Hennepin County. It was licensed as an HMO in 1983 to serve Hennepin County employees and people on the state's PMAP. MHP currently has 30,000 members in four counties, including 6,000 Hennepin County employees and 24,000 people in the state's PMAP. About 1,500 MHP members have selected IHB as their primary care provider, making the IHB the largest community health provider in the MHP network.

Prior to managed care, the county provided services through the county hospital located in the heart of Minneapolis. By absorbing other hospitals in the vicinity, the county hospital grew into the Hennepin County Medical Center (HCMC) with a campus covering a six-block area. HCMC has 450 inpatient beds, a regional trauma center, and numerous outpatient specialty clinics. HCMC provides extended care to people in 37 nursing homes. It also serves as a teaching hospital with residency programs. HCMC has a $320 million annual budget, which includes a $17 million subsidy from county property taxes. Hennepin Faculty Associates (HFA) is a nonprofit, private corporation which provides the staff for HCMC and the clinics owned by them and also contracts with other clinics. Thus, the Hennepin County health system has three parts: HCMC, HFA, and MHP.

There has been a long history of association between community health centers and the county hospital. HCMC helped IHB get started, loaning the clinic its first physician who is still on the IHB staff today. Historically, HCMC has served as the primary referral for IHB patients. In 1995 there were 546 admissions from the IHB to HCMC, which was less than 3 percent of the total admissions. During the same period, IHB had 2,400 referrals to HCMC ambulatory services, which constitutes six to seven percent of the outside referral base. Attempting to be responsive to the needs of Indian patients, HCMC employs an Indian Advocate and offers space for traditional healers to perform ceremonies if patients request it. Both the IHB and the other community

Reception desk at the Minneapolis Indian Health Board.

health centers are considered feeder clinics for HCMC. All of them are contracted providers under MHP. HCMC has contracts with a number of plans in addition to MHP, and approximately 50 percent of third party payments come from conventional insurance coverage.

Unlike Medica, both UCare and MHP require that people enrolled in their plans select a primary care provider (PCP). Plan members can only see specialists in the network after they have been referred by their PCP. Thus, PCP's become gatekeepers in the system as well as case managers. PCPs may be paid either on a capitated basis or on a fee-for-service basis. However, they won't be paid at all unless the member has selected them as a PCP. For example, if a person who has coverage from MHP and has selected a PCP from one of the HCMC clinics comes to IHB for care, the IHB will not be paid by MHP. [4]

Enrolling Members and Designating Primary Care Providers

According to Minnesota laws and regulations, only county offices can enroll people in the state-funded health plans. The county tries to inform people who qualify for MA, GA, or Minnesota Care about their options. They hold a class at which each HMO can present information about its plan; however, few people attend. They send a brochure to all who qualify, however, few people read it. Many people do not exercise their rights to choose a plan, so the state tries to allocate those people to available plans in a fair way. When a plan receives a default assignment, they assign the new member to a primary care provider (PCP).

Quite often, the people who receive care at the IHB have been assigned a PCP at a different location. The patient

---

[4] For those who have a hard time remembering acronyms, this sentence means: "If a person who has coverage from Metropolitan Health Plan (MHP) and has selected a primary care provider (PCP) from one of the Hennepin County Medical Center (HCMC) clinics comes to the Indian Health Board (IHB) for care, the Indian Health Board (IHB) will not be paid by Metropolitan Health Plan (MHP)."

can request that the plan change their PCP to the IHB. For plans in which the IHB receives a capitated payment, the PCP must be changed to the IHB prior to the 10th day of the month, or the IHB will not receive any payment for that month. Even when the IHB assists patients in changing their PCPs, the plan does not always do the paperwork to assure that IHB will receive payment. Tracking systems and followup are required for IHB to assure that they will be paid. While IHB can assist patients in changing their PCPs, patients cannot change health plans at the clinic. They must return to their county social worker to change health plans. Since some plans pay IHB better than other plans, it would be in the IHB interests to have their patients enrolled in the highest paying plans. However, most staff do not even know which plan pays the best and there is no attempt to recruit patients into that or any other plan.

Negotiating Contracts With Health Plans

In Minnesota, there is little room to negotiate contracts between health plans and providers. The state fixes the benefit package and the capitation rates that it pays to health plans. The state requires that the health plans pay at least the state Medicaid fee schedule to providers. And the state approves the prototype contracts between plans and providers.

For the most part, IHB has had to approach the PMAP health plans operating in Hennepin County and ask for a provider contract. The fact that IHB is accredited by the

Joint Commission on Accreditation of Healthcare Organizations (JCAHO) makes it fairly easy for them to gain acceptance by the health plans. Each health plan has a different credentialling process for providers, so the credentials must be submitted in the required format and approved before a contract is offered.

All the contracts between IHB and the Health Plans differ slightly. The majority of the contract defines the relationship between the two organizations and the process for conflict resolution. One of the IHB contracts offers capitated payments, but there is no risk. The other contracts are fee-for-service with the rate set at 10–15 percent above the state Medicaid fee schedule, which is still nearly 50 percent below the cost of doing business. Contracts are presented by the health plans on a "take it or leave it basis." There is no process for negotiating rates or provisions. IHB would like to negotiate not only the rates, but also such things as reimbursement for transportation services provided to clients. However, they regard themselves as too small to get the attention of health plans.

Federally Qualified Health Centers and Cost Based Reimbursement

One disincentive for negotiating more favorable contracts is that the IHB is a Federally Qualified Health Center (FQHC) entitled by federal law to receive cost based reimbursement. The law creating FQHCs was passed in 1990, five years after Minnesota received its first 1115 waiver to create a Medicaid managed care program in Hennepin County. The Executive Director of IHB, worked for two years with the National Association of Community Health Centers (NACHC) and Senator Chaffee to develop the FQHC legislation and advocate for its passage. She saw this as one of the few ways to protect urban Indian clinics, community health centers, and tribally-operated programs that depend on Medicaid as a major source of income. When the legislation was enacted, IHB became the first FQHC in Minnesota and one of the first in the country.

The State of Minnesota was not happy about the FQHC legislation. Because the federal match for Medicaid is only 50 percent in Minnesota, the state had to absorb 50 percent of the additional payments to FQHCs. The state believed that it could serve the same patients for less money by enrolling them in health plans that would assign them to mainstream (non-FQHC) providers. So, when the State of Minnesota applied for another 1115 waiver in 1995, they proposed to eliminate FQHCs. As a compromise measure, they agreed to change the FQHCs to essential community providers (ECPs) and to provide full-cost funding during a three year phaseout of ECPs. While individual ECPs can only keep their full-cost reimbursement for three years, the entire phaseout process is expected to take five years.[5]

During the phaseout period, the state uses a rather complicated system of "settling up" with ECPs. Here is how it works. During the contract year, the ECP receives reimbursement from health plans at the rates established in their contracts. At the end of the contract year (June 30), IHB prepares a cost report and an audit report which have to be submitted by November 30. There are two ways that costs can be calculated, using the HCFA Form 222 or Form 242. A form is filed with the Medicare fiscal intermediary, which in turn sets the rates for Medicaid. The state has to verify all patient charges that IHB has billed to PMAP health plans. Then the state sends a check to IHB for the difference between what was paid by the health plans and the cost approved by Medicare. In the past, this process has taken approximately three years! For IHB, the amount of the "settle up" is approximately $300,000 to $400,000 per

---

[5]The state of Minnesota is treating Tribes more favorably than the urban Indian clinic. The state attributes this difference to the sovereign status of Tribes; however, most observers believe that the motivation is derived from a proposed Memorandum of Agreement (MOA) between the Indian Health Service (IHS) and the Health Care Financing Administration (HCFA) in which the federal government proposes to pay a 100 percent FMAP (federal match) for Medicaid patients who are served in tribally-operated facilities.

year. Neither the state nor the federal governments pay interest on this money during the lengthy settle-up period.

Both IHB and the health plans know that the IHB will eventually receive full-cost reimbursement. There is no incentive for health plans to pay more when they know that the state and federal government will pay whatever the plans do not pay. Because of the delay in receiving the "settle up," the IHB has a stronger incentive to increase its compensation from the health plans, but it is not seen as a matter of survival until the ECP status ends.

How Managed Care Changed the Way IHB Does Business

While IHB has not added staff to deal with the additional demands of managed care, it has had to change its way of doing business.

Operationally, it is important to have systems which track funding sources, referrals and payments in a different way than was used with more conventional insurance. Every time a patient enters the clinic, the registration process includes using the state's Electronic Verification System (EVS) which is accessed by dialing various telephone numbers to check whether the patient is receiving publicly funded health care and to know the health plan in which they are enrolled. If the Health Plan requires assignment of a PCP, then it must be determined whether IHB is the PCP. If not,

Diabetes clinic waiting area, Hennepin County Medical Center.

the admissions personnel assist the patient in transferring the PCP to the IHB. All of these transactions must be logged so that there is a record in case payment is not received from the health plan. Information is updated in the computer for each visit at the registration desk.

If the patient requires specialty care, hospitalization or tests that are not available at IHB, then they must be referred to providers who are part of the network for the health plan in which they are enrolled. A patient care coordinator is responsible for making these appointments, which usually take about 20 minutes per transaction. The physicians must be aware of the patient's health plan and the required network to develop a treatment plan.

While the IHB has a full-scale quality assurance (QA) program that is required for JCAHO accreditation, each health plan can require different additional QA reports. The clinic administrator tells the story of the time the state Department of Human Services decided to audit a health plan which in turn had to choose four clinics with which they contract to review. On the day of the audit, 10 "people in suits" showed up at IHB. They all saw that the situation was slightly ridiculous and decided that half would leave.

The most significant operational change has involved the billing department. IHB employs a certified public accountant (CPA) to submit bills and prepare the reports that are needed to receive the FQHC/ECP settle up. The first time the IHB received its settle up, the check arrived with no audit trail. The clinic requested the information and found that a state programming error had resulted in a shortage. Frequently, health plans make errors in their payment processes, and IHB has to identify the source of the problem and insist on proper payment. IHB has to file special reports requiring documentation to receive incentive pay for things like high-risk prenatal services. For a while, one of the health plans that offered incentive pay for child and teen checkups had a problem with computer software that resulted in the clinic not being paid. Identifying sources of payment and demanding the pay requires both knowledge and persistence. For example, the state law says that health plans must pay for reproductive health services delivered by any provider that the patient chooses. However, IHB has been unable to get the health plans to pay for these services if IHB is not the primary care provider.

Strategies for Survival in a Managed Care Environment

The first strategy that IHB employed was to try to influence the state's policies and legislation with regard to managed care. As early as 1984, IHB began trying to exempt the urban Indian clinics from the state's Medicaid managed care program. Neither the legislature nor state administrators supported this approach. Within one year after the 1115 demonstration project was implemented in Hennepin County, the IHB experienced a deficit.

Recognizing that one reason it was not getting reimbursed was patients were confused and did not select IHB as their primary care provider, the IHB attempted a culturally appropriate strategy to educate patients. At a community feast, IHB staff tried to explain how managed care worked and how to get assigned to the IHB. When the state learned about this, they "slapped the hands" of the IHB. IHB was forbidden from using this strategy to increase their reimbursement for Medicaid patients.

Next, the executive director of IHB, went to work on the national level to help write and advocate for legislation to create Federally Qualified Health Centers (FQHCs) with cost based reimbursement. When the legislation passed, she tried to get the state of Minnesota to modify their laws and regulations to include FQHCs. When the state refused, she enlisted the help of the National Association of Community Health Centers (NACHC). NACHC sent an attorney to Minnesota to convince the state that they had to comply with the federal law. In 1991, Minnesota statutes changed, but by 1995 the state proposed to eliminate FQHCs.

IHB worked closely with the Tribes in Minnesota to develop a consensus on the next strategy. Representing both the Tribes and the urban Indian program, IHB administrators traveled to Baltimore to meet the officials in the Health Care Financing Administration (HCFA). They tried to inform HCFA officials of the federal trust responsibility and the need for Indian health programs. HCFA became involved in getting the state to modify its plan. The compromise involved changing FQHCs to ECPs and creating a three-year phaseout.

IHB is cognizant that it has exhausted its ability to influence the state to create policies that would assure its survival. Even so, there remain misperceptions about the IHB's financial and reimbursement status that must be challenged. For example, the health plan that pays IHB on a capitated basis believes that its payments provide the same income as billable charges, even though it is only 60 percent of the amount. Also, high-level employees of the state's managed care program are unaware that the FQHC settle up is a major source of income for the clinic, composing almost 9 percent of the clinic revenues. Throughout the health care system, there is a general lack of knowledge that 42 percent of IHB patients are uncompensated and that the 10 percent of patients who have third-party resources cannot absorb the discounts for the 45 percent who are Medicaid patients. A key strategy is to correct these misperceptions whenever and wherever they surface.

When the cost-based reimbursement is eliminated in three years, IHB anticipates a $400,000 budget cut. IHB has taken some steps to cut costs. For example, it sends laboratory tests to Hennepin County Medical Center (HCMC) which absorbs the uncompensated costs, rather than the reference laboratory they used previously. HCMC is willing to provide other kinds of support, including donating X-ray equipment.

IHB has also explored alternative funding. Most foundations do not support ongoing operational costs. Also the perceptions of Indian gaming have discouraged foundation funding for Indian programs. Nevertheless, IHB is approaching foundations with specific needs, like a new computer system.

The most promising source of additional funding is increasing the subsidy from local government. The City of Minneapolis is subsidizing 10 other community health centers at the rate of $10 million per year. Another community health center receives 50 percent of its funding from Hennepin County and is administered under the county government. At one point, the Board of Directors of IHB considered turning the clinic over to Hennepin County Medical Center. However, it would probably lose the Indian Health Service funding which composes more than 25 percent of the budget, and this would result in drastic cuts in staff and programs. Instead, IHB has approached the County Commissioners to consider increasing their funding for specific programs and uncompensated care.

There is a high price to seeking additional funding from local government. IHB risks losing its identity as an Indian clinic and becoming more of a neighborhood clinic. Phillips Neighborhood is changing demographically. Some changes are highly visible, like the refugees from Somalia who dress in a distinctive way. In 1990, 24 percent of the people in the neighborhood were Native American and 45 percent were white. While the percentage of Native Americans is remaining constant, the white population is declining and there is an increase in African Americans, Hispanics, Kurdish and Iraqi immigrants, and African refugees. While it has always served everyone who comes through the doors, IHB staff and programs have been designed to serve the Indian community, and they regard it as their clinic. Although 75 percent of the patients are Indians, they compose only 24 percent of the Phillips Neighborhood. If the IHB becomes more of a neighborhood clinic, Indians could be in the minority of patients served.

IHB leadership is also seeking federal solutions. One strategy is to insert wording in existing federal law that would create a status for urban Indian clinics to justify their inclusion in the proposed Memorandum of Agreement between the Indian Health Service (IHS) and the Health Care Financing Administration (HCFA) that would establish a 100 percent federal match for services delivered to Medicaid patients in tribally operated facilities.

Advice to Tribes and Urban Indian Clinics

The following advice comes from a variety of sources, including administrators at the IHB, representatives of health plans, and state managed care officials.

1. It is essential for Indian health programs to monitor trends and external forces at the federal, state, and county levels. Chief Executive Officers must hire the best people they can find to take care of the day-to-day operations so that leadership can focus on networking outside the organization and learning about trends in the larger environment.

2. Managed care is coming. It is important to participate in the planning at the state level and to influence the decisions that shape the program. This participation can be through associations or lobbyists.

3. Indian health programs can't survive the way they were. They must change to become more customer centered to compete with other clinics. Hospitality is important.

4. Prior to negotiating managed care contracts, get as much information as you can about state mandated benefits and your own costs for providing services.

5. Programs that depend on Medicaid managed care income must assure that Indian people are enrolled in health plans for which the Indian health program is a provider.

   If state or county social services are the only place that Medicaid recipients can enroll in health plans, then it is essential that people working in these agencies know about Indian health programs and that they have the information to educate Indian consumers about managed care options.

6. Before beginning new programs, do a cost-benefit analysis. Remember that you cannot be all things for all people, so you have to be selective about the programs you provide.

7. If you need to reduce costs, consider the following strategies:
   - Can you subcontract services for less cost?
   - Can you piggyback with others for more purchasing clout for such things as supplies and telephone service?
   - Can you reduce costs through technology?
   - Can you share staffing with another organization for such things as human resource department?
   - Can you increase your productivity (number of visits per provider per day)?

8. Managed care plans are not the enemy. If you know what you need, you can ask them for help. If they cannot increase their capitation or fee-for-service rates, they may be able to provide some services in kind. For example, they may be able to donate computers.

9. Find mentors and role models.

Chapter 5

Case Study of the Mashantucket Pequot Tribal Nation

The History of a Will to Survive and Thrive

Before the Europeans came to New England, the Mashantucket Pequots numbered 10,000 to 15,000 people living in a 250 square-mile area between the Thames and Pawcatuck Rivers in what is now southeastern Connecticut. They spoke a language in the Algonquian family and engaged in fishing, shell fish gathering, hunting, farming and trading.

European contact was disastrous for the Tribe. In the early 17th century, nearly half the Tribe died from the introduction of diseases. The territory occupied by the Pequots was strategic for controlling the trade of furs and wampum, which was used as money by both Indian Tribes and colonists. English and Dutch settlers were competing for furs and wampum, which created a hostile environment for the

Pequots. Many died in wars. In 1637, the English surrounded the Pequot fort in Mystic, set it on fire and systematically killed all who tried to escape. It is estimated that more than 700 Pequots died in this massacre which lasted only one hour. The Treaty of Hartford in 1638 divided surviving Pequots between the Mohegan and Narragansett Tribes.

Pequots resisted attempts to force their assimilation into other Tribes. Under the leadership of Robin Cassasinamon, sachem from 1637 until his death in 1692, the Mashantucket Pequots resettled in Nameag (New London) and Noank (Groton) in 1650. In 1667, the State of Connecticut created a reservation with approximately 2,500 acres in the area that is now Ledyard. This is the oldest continually occupied reservation in the United States. However, the land dwindled to just 214 acres in 1856, as the state-appointed overseers sold plots without Tribal approval. State laws prohibited economic development, and the Pequots suffered from poverty, poor housing and a lack of services. People left the reservation for employment and better opportunities.

In 1974, the Mashantucket Pequot Tribal Nation reorganized its Tribal government and drafted a Tribal constitution. There were 188 Tribal members. From 1976 until 1983, the Tribe enlisted the help of the Native American Rights Fund (NARF) to seek federal recognition and to reclaim their land. The Mashantucket Pequot Land Claims Settlement Act of 1983 restored federal recognition and began the process of economic development.

Since 1986, the Tribe's gaming operations have grown rapidly. First, the Tribe opened a 2,100-seat bingo hall in 1986. In 1992, the Tribe opened the Foxwoods High Stakes Bingo & Casino, a $60 million facility with 46,000 square feet, employing 2,300 people. The Tribe negotiated an agreement with the State of Connecticut to allow Foxwoods to offer slot machines in 1993. This agreement had a provision that the Tribe would pay the state 25 percent of slot machine revenues; however, the agreement would be nullified if casinos were legalized anywhere else in Connecticut.

The agreement has provided the state with revenues and additional employment at a time when there were cuts in the defense industry which was a mainstay of employment in the state. The agreement was renegotiated in 1994 to allow the nearby Mohegan Tribe to open a casino.

With the addition of slot machines, Foxwoods was expanded in November 1993 to 1.3 million square feet, including a theater complex, restaurants and shops. The Tribe also opened two hotels, with a combined total of 594 rooms. In 1994, the casino was expanded again, making it the largest casino in the country and one of the largest employers in Connecticut, with 10,000 employees and a $220 million a year payroll. In 1995, the casino was expanded again and it set new national records for slot machine revenues. With an average of 45,000 visitors per day, or more than 16 million people per year, the annual revenue sharing payments to the state are expected to exceed $150 million. Currently, the Tribe is spending $350 million to build a 17-story hotel tower and conference center with 917 rooms. To serve the casino, the Tribe has extensive support facilities including a state-of-the-art waste water treatment plant, an extensive police and fire department, roads and parking lots, and shuttle buses.

While revenues from gaming have been reinvested in casino expansion, they have been used also to fund other Tribal facilities and programs, including a child development center and recreational facilities for Tribal members. The Tribe is constructing a $130-million museum and research center. Revenues from gaming have enabled the Tribe to purchase land to begin to restore the reservation to its original size. The Tribe has also built or refurbished housing for Tribal members on the reservation. With jobs and housing, people have returned to the reservation and Tribal enrollment has increased to approximately 450 people.

The Mashantucket Pequot Tribal Nation has diversified its business interests to include hotels and restaurants off the reservation. The Tribe also owns the Pequot River Shipworks, which is building high-speed ferries in New London, Connecticut. Since 1991, the Tribe has operated a revenue-producing pharmaceutical service.

An elected Tribal Council is responsible for all major decisions and activities of the Tribe. The Tribe is organized into two parts. One part includes Tribal government programs, most of which receive some federal funding. The other part is composed of businesses owned by the Tribe. A Tribal manager is responsible for the Tribal governmental programs. Each division of Tribal governmental programs has the oversight of a standing committee of the Tribal Council. The Division of Health and Human Services is responsible for the Indian Health Service (IHS)-funded programs, including a clinic providing direct care and the Contract Health Services. On the business side, each enterprise has a board of directors. The Tribal Council appoints the chair of the board and the chair recommends the other board members for council approval. A majority of board members must be Tribal members. The revenue producing health programs on the business side are under the umbrella of Pequot Pharmaceutical Network (PRxN).

Providing Health Benefits to Tribal Employees

Today managed care is the way that three-fourths of all workers with health benefits receive their health care in the United States. Most businesses with over 5,000 employees are self-insured under the Employee Retirement Income Security Act of 1974 (ERISA), exempting them from state regulation of these employee benefits. So, one might expect that Tribes with a large number of employees would provide health benefits through a self-insured managed care plan.

This case study is about the Mashantucket Pequot Tribal Nation, which has over 12,000 employees, of which about 10,700 qualify for health benefits. With their dependents, nearly 22,000 people are covered. The purchasing power in these numbers allows the Tribe to negotiate special rates with health care providers in the private sector. Tribal members are included in the health benefit plan as well as receiving services funded by the Indian Health Service.

The Mashantucket Pequot Tribal Nation has developed a complex, integrated system of health care delivery. The centerpiece of this system is the Mashantucket Pequot Health Benefit Plan (MPHBP), a managed care plan that is owned, financed, and administered by the Tribe through its Pequot Pharmaceutical Network (PRxN).[6] PRxN also has developed a Pharmacy Network and Remote Distribution[7], which are revenue-producing managed care pharmacy services that are used by the Tribe and marketed to other plans and Tribes. The MPHBP is a point-of-service preferred provider organization (POS-PPO) which has both a Medical PPO and a Dental PPO. While the MPHBP is designed to manage both costs and health care, other aspects of the health care delivery system also contribute to these

---

[6]The term "PRxN" has received a Service Mark from the U. S. Patent Office.
[7]The term "Remote Distribution" has received a Service Mark from the U.S. Patent Office.

Offices of Pequot Pharmaceutical Network, including both the pharmacy for Tribal members and employees, the Pequot Pharmaceutical Network managed care pharmacy plan, and the mail order pharmacy operations.

goals, including Employee Health Services (EHS) and Con-tract Health Services (CHS), which are in the Tribe's Department of Health and Human Services, a different administrative division from PRxN.

Saving money for the Tribe and providing quality health services for Tribal members and employees have been the main goals of the MPHBP. However, components of the plan, including the pharmacy, can be revenue producing for the Tribe when they are marketed to other Tribes and plans. Can Tribes make money on managed care? Yes.

Development of the Mashantucket Pequot Health Benefit Plan

In 1983 when the Tribe received federal recognition, it was anticipated that the Indian Health Service (IHS) would provide some funding for health services. While the Tribe had only 188 members at that time, there were 2,000 people in the service area of New London County eligible for IHS. These included American Indians relocated from Maine and other parts of New England in the 1950s to work in defense and ship building industries in Connecticut.

In 1986 the Tribe began the first phase of a health planning process that looked at the health status and use of health services by Tribal members. Two significant findings came out of that study. First, it found that many tribal members had multiple chronic health problems and that they had already developed relationships with specialists in the private sector. This meant that any health plan would have to consider their freedom to choose their own providers. The second significant finding was that among the Indian population served, 45 percent of the resources were spent on medications, compared to 10 percent in most other populations. These findings were so intriguing that the Tribe obtained a second grant to investigate whether this pattern was found in other Tribes. One other Tribe participated in the study and the findings were the same. This gave rise to the idea that controlling pharmacy costs was the best way to reduce health care costs.

When gaming started in 1986, the Tribe entered into a five year agreement with the Penobscot Tribe of Maine to comanage the bingo operations. Initially, the number of tribal employees was small. The Tribe subscribed to the Indian Member Benefit Fund (IMBF), a medical self-insurance program of 10 Tribes that belonged to the United South and Eastern Tribes. The third-party administrator (TPA), for IMBF was Blue Cross of Tennessee, and claims were paid at Tennessee rates which were considerably lower than Connecticut fees for medical services. Anticipating an expansion in gaming and tribal employment, the Tribe realized that salaries and benefits would become the largest expense. This created an incentive to look at ways to control the costs of health benefits and at the same time create a benefit package that would attract and retain employees. One alternative for reducing costs was to "cut out the middle man"—in this case Blue Cross of Tennessee—and for the Tribe to become its own TPA.

The Tribe looked at alternatives for providing services to tribal members, tribal employees and their dependents. They knew that tribal members wanted the freedom to choose their own providers. One guiding principle was that there should not be a two-tiered system with different levels of benefits. Other principles were quality of care, accessibility, and affordability. The Tribe also had to consider the economic viability of any plan. They asked the questions, "Can we do it ourselves? Can we save money by doing it ourselves?" Later as the plan evolved, they added the criteria of transportability and responsibility.

In 1990, when the Tribe was investigating its options, managed care was already a well-accepted approach for employee benefits. But, the Tribe had only 365 employees and the health care system covered only 3,000 people (2,000 American Indians and dependents). It was difficult for CHS to secure contracts from private providers at that time because the Tribe could not offer volume in exchange for discounts. However, the planning process anticipated growth to covering 25,000 lives. The projections were not unreasonable: By 1996 the plan covered 21,730 lives, and an additional 600 to 700 employees were expected when the new hotel opens in 1997. With these numbers, the Tribe had considerably more purchasing power, particularly at a time when other employment in the state was in decline due to cutbacks in the defense industry.

The Tribe considered a variety of managed care alternatives. It rejected the idea of a closed panel health maintenance organization (HMO) as too restrictive and not compatible with their goals and values. The approach that was found to be most acceptable was a "bridge to managed care" called a "point-of-service preferred provider organization" (POS-PPO). The POS-PPO offers consumers choice at the time they receive service rather than at the time they enroll. The consumers are given financial incentives to use providers who have contracted at discounts within the PPO network. The plan assumes all risk for services

Private clinic about 10 miles from the reservation that provides ambulatory care for Pequot Tribal members and employees under the Pequot Managed Care plan.

provided both within the PPO and out of the network. All providers are paid on a fee-for-service basis.

In July of 1991, the Tribe voted to establish its own plan, the Mashantucket Pequot Health Benefit Plan (MPHBP) with the Tribe serving as the TPA. The previous year, First American Pharmaceutical Network was established by the Tribe to provide pharmacy benefits under the plan and to be marketed outside the Tribe. Later, the name was changed to Pequot Pharmaceutical Network (PRxN), and all of the business enterprises associated with the Health Benefit Plan, including the TPA, were brought under the management of PRxN.

For quick startup, the Tribe kept the benefit package the same as the IMBF plan and contracted with a firm for two years to establish a system for the TPA and train employees. However, the startup was not easy. The Tribe inherited a $1 million backlog of claims from IMBF. At the same time that the Tribe was trying to establish systems and hire and train employees, it was also coping with rapid growth. Within six months after startup, the new casino opened and the number of employees went from 365 to over 2,300. The growth has never slowed. In the two years after the contract ended with the firm that established the TPA, the number of tribal employees working for the TPA grew from 7 to 35. In 1995 the plan organized a network of 334 contracted licensed dentists covering eastern Connecticut, Rhode Island, and southeastern Massachusetts. The Remote Distribution operations of the Pequot pharmacy has grown from filling fewer than 25,000 prescriptions in 1992 to more than 175,000 in 1996.

Since the plan was initiated in 1991, a new benefits package has been developed. Starting on January 1, 1997, employees have been required to contribute to the cost of the plan. Under the Employee Retirement Income Security Act of 1974 (ERISA), the employee contributions must be kept in a separate fund.

Benefit Package

The Mashantucket Pequot Health Benefit Plan (MPHBP) has a defined benefit package that is described in a handbook given to all who are enrolled. Those who are enrolled are all Mashantucket Pequot Tribal members, eligible employees of the Tribe and their dependents, and people who are eligible for IHS and reside in the service area and have close social and economic ties to the Tribe. There is a 90-day waiting period after enrollment before benefits begin. Employees are not covered for pre-existing conditions until six months after enrolling in the plan; however, they can receive medications for those pre-existing conditions with no out-of-pocket expenditure during the waiting period.

The benefit package includes medical, hospital, dental, pharmacy, laboratory and X-ray, optometry, mental health, and alcohol abuse treatment services. It includes some services not usually found in health plans, such as speech therapy, allergy testing, acupuncture, home health care, durable medical equipment, and orthodontics.

Tribal employees can choose from two medical plans: Traditional Plan, or Pequot Options Plan. The Pequot Options Plan is the PPO.

The Traditional Plan allows employees to seek health care outside the PPO. Those who choose the Traditional Plan have a $250 deductible per person or $750 deductible per family. They pay approximately 20 percent of usual and customary charges for a maximum out-of-pocket expenditure of $1,000 per individual or $3,000 per family.

Those who choose the PPO do not have any deductible and many preventive services are provided at no cost to the consumer, such as annual physical exams, immunizations (including influenza) and well-child visits. Also, there is no copay for maternity care, X-rays and laboratory, diagnostic procedures, surgery, hospital care, and home health care. Some services offered by the PPO, such as outpatient physician visits, have a $10 copay.

For both types of plans, the Pequot Pharmaceutical Network fills all prescriptions at no charge to the consumer.

The dental benefits plan is managed separately from the medical benefits plan. All dental copays and deductibles are separate from and in addition to all medical copays and deductibles. The dental benefits are similar for both the PPO network and people seeking care outside the network. In both cases, the consumer pays 50 to 80 percent for most services and there is an annual benefit maximum of $1,500. The incentive to use the dental PPO is that lower prices have been negotiated, and the plan is actively involved in quality assurance, so that the amount the consumer pays is expected to be lower than using providers who are not part of the PPO.

At the time of this report, the mental health and substance/alcohol benefits were similar between the PPO and the non-PPO options. There is an incentive to use the tribally contracted Employee Assistance Program (EAP). When plan members use the EAP, their lifetime maximum is $12,500, compared to $5,000 when they do not use the EAP. However, this could change with federal legislation requiring mental health services to be on parity with medical services.

Vision care services have not yet been organized into a PPO. Because optometry represents less than one percent of health expenditures, it is the last element the Tribe has brought into the managed care arena. The benefits plan allows for annual eye exams with a $30 maximum, and an annual allowance of $50 for lenses, $30 for frames every 24 months, and $80 for contact lenses annually. These are negotiated rates that often cover the full cost.

Third-Party Administration

The third-party administrator (TPA) adjudicates claims and pays providers. Typically, the TPA is paid an administrative fee on a capitated basis. So the TPA would receive a negotiated rate per member per month. Rather than paying this to an outside agency, the Mashantucket Pequot Tribe decided to manage its plan through an in-house TPA. This not only keeps the money and employment within the Tribe, but it also assures that the TPA is responsive to the needs of tribal members and employees.

In 1996, the Mashantucket Pequot TPA had 35 employees and a highly sophisticated computer system. The turnaround time from when a claim is received to when it is paid is seven days. Initially, claims averaged a 70-day turnaround due to the backlog in claims inherited from the previous plan. Investment in computers and personnel has made the system

extremely efficient, performing well above the contractual requirements that providers be paid in 45 days on clean claims.

After claims are received they are scanned into the computer so that further processing can be accomplished using
computer images in a paperless setting. The documents are
indexed so that they can be retrieved on the computer in
conjunction with a member's file. If consumers or providers call to ask about claims, the customer service representative can call up the document on the computer rather
than searching for it in hardcopy files. Claims adjudicators
review the claims in the computer files to assure that the
person is covered under the plan, that the service is included in the plan, and that the bill has not already been
paid. The claims adjudicator can authorize payment on the
computer which is programmed to print checks to the providers. A percentage of the payments are withheld elec-
tronically for review by an auditor. The auditors not only
review the files for accuracy, but they also run an automated
program which checks for errors, such as the wrong diagnosis code. After the auditor's review, withheld payments are
released, and the checks are generated by the computer.

The computer system requires ongoing maintenance to
add and remove plan members and to enter discount rates
for contracted providers. The TPA employs a case manager
who serves as a claims adjudicator, as well as managing care
and negotiating rates for high-cost services that are provided outside the PPO.

Medical PPO Management

Since the beginning of the plan, the Tribe has contracted for certain management elements of the Medical PPO. The Tribe wanted to retain control over most aspects of the PPO including paying claims, but it also wanted to use existing networks or independent practice associations (IPAs) to provide a broad panel of physicians in the PPO. After going out to bid, the Tribe selected Physician Health Services (PHS), a company with 15 years of experience and an existing network serving one-third of all employees in the region.

The Tribe pays PHS a capitated monthly service fee. This is not a premium, it is not taxable, and it has no risk. The per member per month rate pays PHS to provide specific services. These include recruitment, credentialing, negotiations, and contracting with physicians. While PHS came to the contract with a large physician network, the Tribe required that the network be expanded to include a three-state area. PHS provides a fee schedule to the TPA which is then used in paying claims to the providers.

PHS serves other functions that are typically associated with managed care. These include precertification of hospital stays, continued stay review, discharge planning, precertification of costly outpatient procedures, and case management for people with major illnesses, chronic illnesses, and high-cost care. PHS also performs quality assurance programs with providers.

While PHS performs many management functions, the Tribe reserves the right to add providers to the PPO or to delete those providers who are not responsive to the needs of Indian people. The Tribe also has control over standards of care, such as length of stay in hospitals after deliveries.

Physicians in the PPO have very limited risk. If a primary care provider does not follow the standards set forth in their contract with PHS, then they are fined and the Mashantucket Pequot Tribe receives a rebate.

Dental PPO Management

The Mashantucket Pequot Health Benefit Plan has one of the best organized Dental PPOs in Connecticut. The cost per member per month is approximately $30. The benefits are limited, and therefore costs are relatively predictable. The plan provides savings because it pays at the 70th percentile of charges rather than the 90th percentile that is typical of traditional dental insurance. Through utilization review by a dentist requiring X-rays of completed work, there is less unnecessary dental work performed, patients receive higher quality of care, and payments are not made until work is completed. The overhead is low: the Pequot dental TPA can process claims on an average of 22,000 people with only two adjudicators aided by electronic systems.

When the dental PPO was started, marketing materials were sent to 2,000 dentists in the state, including all those who were treating people enrolled in the Mashantucket Pequot Health Benefit Plan. Initially, dentists were reluctant to join a managed care plan. Only 10 percent of those who received marketing materials signed contracts. But these 200 dentists were well distributed geographically and provided the corps needed to start the plan. Other dentists joined after a court ruled that the indemnity dental plans could not keep them from joining this plan. Today there are 334 licensed dentists in Connecticut, Rhode Island, and Massachusetts in the MPHBP dental PPO.

Similar to the medical PPO, the dental PPO contracted with another organization for some of the management activities. Insurance Dentists of America (IDOA), a firm in California with a network of over 35,000 dentists, provides credentialing, quality assurance, and monitoring costs of services.

One successful aspect of the dental PPO has been an Advisory Committee that includes dentists contracted under the plan. The dentists have been able to better understand how the plan works and to communicate this information to their peers. The Advisory Committee has increased the level of trust between the Mashantucket Pequot Tribe and the professional community.

Pharmacy Services

The Mashantucket Pequot Tribe offers two types of pharmacy services: prescriptions filled by the Pequot pharmacy, called "Remote Distribution"; and a national network of

Prescription processing for on-site Pharmacy and Remote Distribution.

private pharmacies that provide discount services, called "Pequot Pharmaceutical Network." While both of these services are provided to members of the Mashantucket Pequot Health Benefit Plan, they are also marketed outside the Tribe as a revenue-producing activity. Initially, the Pequots planned to market this service to other Tribes, based on research showing that other Tribes were spending as much as 45 percent of their health care resources on purchasing medicines. However, the demand for these services has grown to include not only Tribes, but also managed care plans, ERISA plans, hospice programs, Medicaid and Workers Compensation.

Pharmacy Operations—Remote Distribution

The pharmacy on the Pequot reservation fills 1,200 to 1,400 prescriptions per day. It serves about 200–300 people as walk-ins each day. About 40 percent of the people served come as walk-ins, usually tribal members or tribal employees. If their prescriptions are not called in ahead of time, they may wait 20 minutes for their medicines, including counseling from a registered pharmacist. Approximately 60 percent of the services are provided by mail or Federal Express, with an average turnaround time of 48 hours.

The pharmacy maintains three separate inventories. One inventory contains drugs purchased off the federal schedule, and these can only be used to fill prescriptions for members of the Pequot Tribe and other IHS-eligible Native Americans. The second inventory contains medicines purchased at a discount through a wholesale firm, and these are used to provide drugs under non-tribal managed care plans. The third inventory contains samples which are used to fill prescriptions written by physicians employed by the Pequot tribal health clinic. The MPHBP has a preferred drug list and a generic mandate.

Computers are used to track all prescriptions. When prescriptions are received by mail, information is entered into the computer, which generates bar codes that can be scanned throughout the process to pull up information or enter additional information. Computers are programmed to send information to managed care plans, including the Pequot Pharmaceutical Network, and to receive authorization to bill the plan for the prescription. When that authorization is received, the computer automatically prints a sheet that contains a peel-off label for the medicine, warning labels, a mailing label, counseling information about the drug for the patient, a receipt and a refill card. The prescription is filled by technicians using automated systems for counting pills. The completed order is reviewed by a registered pharmacist who signs the order with a quality pledge. Orders are then packed for shipping. Federal Express is used for orders over $200 or containing controlled substances or where requested. Federal Express picks up orders 3 to 4 times per day and provides online tracking with a computer at the Pequot pharmacy to answer any consumer questions.

The volume of prescriptions is so large for the storage space that drugs are reordered twice a day using a computerized inventory program. Drugs are delivered by the wholesaler the day after they are ordered. The Pequot Pharmacy employs eight registered pharmacists (including two in administrative positions) and more than 20 nationally certified pharmacy technicians. The Tribe pays for training and testing of pharmacy technicians. In addition, there is a large data entry and account services staff. There are two shifts of employees. Security is tight throughout the building, including cameras that record activities within the pharmacy.

The Remote Pharmacy makes money by charging clients a flat administrative fee in addition to the cost of drugs. Discount rates on drugs, use of automation and computers, low overhead costs, and quality service makes the Remote Pharmacy competitive both within Connecticut and throughout the nation. Particularly, for people with medications for chronic diseases, the Remote Pharmacy can provide drugs at considerable savings over using a local retail pharmacy.

Pharmacy Network

The Pharmacy Network includes about 30,000 retail pharmacies, including most of the largest nationwide chains, that are contracted to provide their products at a discount to members of the Pequot Pharmacy Network. Various Tribes and managed care plans contract with the Pharmacy Network to adjudicate and pay their claims. When the Pharmacy Network has a new client, they contact retail pharmacies in that area of the country and invite them to join the network. This is done by sending them a standard contract which they can sign and return. The contract calls for payment based on an average wholesale price less a discount plus a fee.

The Pharmacy Network has a computerized claims adjudication system. The participating pharmacies have computers which send information to the Pequot Pharmacy Network computer. The PRxN computer automatically checks 20 kinds of information and then issues an electronic authori-

Computers provide online authorization to pharmacies throughout the country linked to Pequot Pharmaceutical Network.

zation to the participating pharmacy in a few seconds. The kinds of information automatically checked by the computer include whether the individual is enrolled in the plan, whether the plan provides coverage for this medication, the amount of copay required of the patient, and the amount that the plan will pay to the retail pharmacy. For hospices and workers compensation plans, the pharmacy computer programs are able to manage prescriptions by diagnosis. The computers can also check to see whether it is time for a prescription refill and whether there may be drug interactions with other prescriptions.

The computer also generates consolidated bills to each of the clients. And the computer calculates the payments to each retail pharmacy and generates preprinted checks. The Pharmacy Network bills the Mashantucket Pequot Health Benefit Plan Trust Fund for prescriptions provided to tribal members and employees. And the Pharmacy Network pays the Pharmacy Operations Remote Pharmacy for prescriptions they have filled, both under the Pequot plan and for people enrolled in other plans that have contracted with the Pharmacy Network and had their prescriptions filled through the Remote Pharmacy.

The Pharmacy Network serves 70 clients (purchasers) that cover 2 million eligible members. About 45 percent of the revenues are generated from the Mashantucket Pequot Health Benefit Plan, while 55 percent of revenues are generated by outside clients.

Financing the Plan

In 1995, after a decade of maintaining the same rates without adjustment for the ongoing inflation in medical costs, the Tribe raised the monthly fees for the Mashantucket Pequot Health Benefit Plan to $179 for a single person and $535 for families. However, these rates are expected to be reduced in April 1997. Starting January 1, 1997, the Tribe began requiring employee contributions.

Two trust funds have been established in the PRxN to receive funding for the Mashantucket Pequot Health Benefit Plan. Tribal government, Foxwoods Casino and other tribal businesses pay into one trust fund for their employees. The employer contribution for single employees is $159 per month and for employees with families it is $495 per month. The Tribe's General Fund pays the premium to the Trust Fund for tribal members who are not tribal employees. Employee contributions are put into a separate ERISA Trust Fund. Employees contribute $5 per week for single employees and $10 per week for those with family benefits. Both trust funds are used to pay for services provided under the health plan and for administrative costs; however, ERISA rules place limitations on the types of expenses that can be funded from employee contributions.

The 90-day waiting period for benefits to start coincides with the probationary period for tribal employees. They are not allowed to use any benefits during the probationary period, but they are accruing benefits that can be used after they pass the probationary period. This system not only gives time to enroll the employee in the benefit plan, but it also means that premiums start one month before benefits start. This makes it a truly prepaid system and assists with cash flow.

Money in the trust funds is used to pay the management fees for the TPA and the Pharmacy Network, which in turn is used to pay salaries of tribal employees working in those areas, as well as other fixed administrative costs. When the

TPA and the Pharmacy Network pay claims for services provided to MPHBP members, they bill the trust funds to cover the costs of those claims.

ERISA requires that the trust funds maintain a reserve to cover claims that have been incurred but not reported (IBNR). This budget line item, IBNR is calculated using a formula that results in a reserve of several million dollars.

The plan purchases individual stop-loss insurance to cover claims over $200,000 per event in a year. The rule of thumb is that stop-loss should be 10 percent of medical exposure. However, the larger the pool of covered persons, the safer the risk. Coverage for stop-loss insurance was put out to bid by the Tribe, but initially there was little competition for the contract. Most insurers were not interested in covering Indians because of their sovereignty, perceived higher risk, and possibly discrimination. One company did agree to insure the Tribe, and a long-term relationship developed.

Although most of the tribal health activities are within the scope of the contract with the Indian Health Service and would thus qualify for Federal Tort Claims Act coverage, the Tribe purchases liability insurance, including malpractice insurance. The Tribe also requires pharmacists to carry their own insurance.

The Tribe bears all risk for the plan. This means that if aggregate claims exceed the amount in the trust funds, then the Tribe must pay the difference from its General Fund. This situation has not occurred. However, at the beginning

Indian Health Service funded clinic on the Pequot Reservation.

when there was no actuarial experience to set rates in the rapidly growing environment, the reserve account was depleted to a level so low that the trust fund borrowed from the Tribe's General Fund until higher premium rates could repay the loan and build up a substantial reserve.

Indian Health Service Interface

In addition to the Mashantucket Pequot Health Benefit Plan, the Tribe has a small tribally operated clinic, similar to other Tribes. The clinic employs two physicians, support staff, a community health nurse and two outreach workers. These services are under the auspices of Tribal Governmental Programs, rather than the Pequot Pharmaceutical Network. The clinic does not have a pharmacy because those services are provided through the Pequot Pharmaceutical Network. The clinic provides direct services to people who are eligible for the Indian Health Service (IHS). About 50 percent of the patients are Pequot tribal members and the other 50 percent are enrolled in other Tribes. Approximately 1,100 people are registered at the clinic, although an estimated 4,000 are eligible. Among those registered, about 400 are eligible for direct care only and use this as their primary health care provider.

There is no financial incentive for tribal members to use the clinic instead of a private provider under the PPO. Sometimes, people use the clinic because it is more convenient for urgent care, such as having a sick child examined. Sometimes Tribal members use the clinic staff to help them understand the diagnosis and treatment plan given by the private physician under the PPO. The clinic's medical director has a very personal style of patient advocacy, making house calls to the elders and even accompanying patients into surgery to provide moral support. The clinic does not bill third-party payers. Thus, the plan does not pay for services delivered at the clinic.

While the Pequot Tribe has a Title I model contract under P.L. 93-638, the contract specifies that there is cost sharing between the Tribe and the Indian Health Service. Under the contract, the Tribe receives the appropriation at the beginning of the fiscal year and issues one report and audit at the end of the fiscal year. The IHS provides about $780,000 in funding, and the Tribe contributes about twice that much. The funds are comingled, and most of the tribal health activities are covered in the contract. The contract serves as a way to signal that these activities are being conducted within the government-to-government relationship and under the control of a sovereign Indian nation. While the MPHBP is exempt from state regulation under ERISA for employees, it is the IHS contract that makes the plan exempt from state regulation for tribal members who are not employees.

The federal funding for Contract Health Services (CHS) is approximately $74,000 and the Tribe also contributes money to the CHS budget. The Tribe has defined eligibility for CHS as being a member of a federally recognized Tribe, and living on the Pequot Reservation or within the New London County Service Area, and having "close social and economic ties" to the Mashantucket Pequot Tribal Nation. "Close social and economic ties" means that the individual is married to a tribal member or is employed by the Tribe. CHS also applies to full-time students who are living outside the service area and Indian foster children living on the reservation. CHS funding can also be used for maternity care for pregnant women when the child is expected to be eligible for CHS.

To make health benefits free of cost to tribal members, the Tribe uses CHS funding to pay for all allowable expenses that are not covered by the plan, including employee copays, deductibles, costs in excess of annual or lifetime benefit limits, and transportation outside the area. Some services are excluded from both the plan and CHS, such as plastic surgery, treatment for infertility, and dental implants. When CHS pays for services not covered by the plan, they usually get the same discounted rate that the Tribe uses under the plan.

The Department of Health and Human Services, under Tribal Governmental Programs, also includes other health programs. There is an air quality program that is responsible for testing carbon dioxide and oxygen flow at all tribal facilities, including the Foxwoods Casino. The food and sanitation program is responsible for inspecting the 16 restaurants and food courts in the casino complex.

Managing Costs Through Employee Health Services

The Employee Health Services (EHS) program was started in 1994 when the Tribe had about 9,000 employees. The Tribe realized that they could save money by providing pre-employment physicals and required immunizations through direct services rather than contracting these services.

EHS is located off the reservation in the same building as Foxwood's Human Resources, where applicants for employment are screened. Pre-employment physicals include a health profile, an exam by a physician and a PPD (tuberculosis) screening. While drug testing is contracted out, specimen collection is done at the EHS office with the required chain of custody precautions. After employment, EHS provides employees with Hepatitis B vaccines, tetanus shots, annual PPDs, flu shots, and rabies vaccines.

The pre-employment physicals identify conditions which may put the person at a health risk for a particular job. If the EHS physician finds that a person may not be able to fully participate in the work in the job description, that individual is referred to his/her primary care provider for clearance. This assures a healthier workforce, which could result in lower costs to the MPHBP.

In 1995, EHS started a satellite clinic at the casino. Open 24-hours per day and staffed by five occupational health nurses, the satellite clinic serves as a triage center for employees. This has reduced the number of ambulance calls to take employees to the hospital. By counseling employees to use primary care providers under the PPO, the number of employee visits to hospital emergency rooms has declined dramatically.

Managing Growth

Managing growth has been an ongoing challenge that includes hiring and training employees, developing new systems, and adding computers and other types of automation. In four years, the PRxN went from three personal computers to 120 workstations and four complicated systems. All of this requires space. On the small Mashantucket Pequot Reservation, there are no unoccupied buildings in which to expand, so this often means crowded working conditions. Moving to facilities off the reservation is not an option because Tribal sovereignty would be compromised.

The Tribe has faced the challenges of managing growth by hiring well-qualified, energetic, loyal, and committed people at all levels. There are so few tribal members that most positions cannot be filled by tribal members. However, the Tribe has initiated some policies that try to keep control of decision making within the Tribe. For example, it is required that the Tribe be represented by a tribal member at all meetings including those that involve travel.

Growth in employment opportunities and the availability of quality housing has resulted in many tribal members returning to the reservation. Also there are more people applying for tribal membership. Social and family services are available to assist Tribal members with the transition of moving to the reservation. About 50 percent of the tribal members are under 18 years old. The Tribe provides a child development center for young children and pays the full cost of education for all tribal members who want to go to college. In this way the Tribe is trying to prepare its young people to take on the future leadership and management roles within the Tribe.

With rapid growth, there can be conflicts. Success can create pressures that divide families. The Tribe has initiated Peacemakers, a culturally based conflict resolution process designed to maintain harmony. Two members from each tribal family are on the Peacemakers Council. Decisions of this council are considered final. One advantage of this approach is that it frees the Tribal Council from dealing with personnel grievances and other matters which could be divisive and time consuming.

Traditional Healing

Traditional healing is a complex subject for the Mashantucket Pequot Tribe. For nearly 300 years the Tribe was subject to oppressive measures which attempted to prohibit people from speaking their language and engaging in their own cultural practices. Tribal members who were required to live with the Narragansett or Mohegan Tribes learned about their traditions and healing practices. Many tribal members have returned to the reservation from urban areas where they were removed from traditional knowledge. Tribal members who have sought alcohol and drug abuse treatment from programs with an American Indian focus have returned to the reservation with cultural models that have been derived from other Tribes. Nevertheless, the Tribe recognizes the need for spiritual guidance and there is at least one elder in the Tribe who has traditionally provided spiritual leadership.

Most of the traditional healing activities within the Tribe take place at Tall Pines, a log house on the reservation that serves as a meeting place for Alcoholics Anonymous (AA) and other groups of Tribal members. Within this setting, there are talking circles and a focus on reaffirmation of identity. Native health practitioners and spiritual leaders come from Canada and other places to share with tribal members. Sweats are also conducted at a different location. While the Tribe sponsors these activities and provides a meeting place, there is no attempt to integrate traditional healing into the MPHBP or the health clinic.

Advice to Other Tribes

The following advice about starting a managed care enterprise comes from many people in various levels of administration of the PRxN:

1. Find tribal members with health knowledge to serve on the board of directors of tribal health enterprises. Tribal leaders need to be informed and need to keep tribal members informed.

2. It is difficult to know who to trust for advice. Consultants tend to be self-serving and costly. If you are going to start a TPA, try to visit other TPAs to see how their systems are organized. This is difficult because they may view you as a competitor. However, if you tell them that you are only going to serve Indian populations, they

may be more receptive to sharing information with you. The management team at PRxN is happy to share their experience and knowledge with other Tribes.

3. Take time to plan. Identify needs and opportunities. Do feasibility studies. Target the market you are seeking to penetrate. Be flexible and creative in designing systems. Use a team approach so that you get many perspectives.

4. Start with experienced staff rather than trusting consultants to design processes and train staff. Hire people who have expertise in both the private health system and the federal government. It is important to know the federal system to make it work for you.

5. Decide what the Tribe can do successfully and what services and expertise the Tribe needs to obtain through contracts with other organizations.

6. Do your homework. Don't just listen to one approach. Everyone seems to be selling their goods or services—they embellish the good and don't tell you the bad aspects of their products. Companies will always try to sell you the most sophisticated software on the market—you need to question the application and workflow. When purchasing goods or services from consultants or vendors, ask for a list of their clients. Don't let them steer you to a happy client they have selected. Interview clients whose operations are similar to yours and go look at their operations.

7.   Managed care systems require a huge investment in technology and learning to use it. Because technology changes so rapidly, the Tribe must keep investing in replacement technology, upgrading equipment and training. As computer needs change, it is important to consider using a single platform so that systems can be integrated. Do not buy software with capability beyond your needs.

8.   A dental PPO is a good place to start a managed care enterprise. It is less complicated than a medical PPO, it does not require big investments in computers, and it takes only a few employees to manage claims. The Dental PPO should be under the direction of a dentist who can relate to other dentists in the private sector. A dental assistant who understands terms can be trained to handle claims. The most effective way to save money for clients is to demand that dental work be completed before payment by reviewing final X-rays. In organizing a dental PPO, you must be fair to dentists, but watch what they do!

9.   If you are starting a TPA and taking over claims management from another business, negotiate the conditions of the transition. Don't just end the previous plan without defining how claims received but not paid will be handled.

10. Customer service is important to keep consumers, providers, and purchasers happy. The most knowledgeable employees, who have worked as claims ad-

justers, should be assigned to customer service. By scanning claims, all information is available in computer files, and most decisions can be made on the first telephone call without requiring any return calls.

11. Maintain the privacy of clients and consumers—do not let tribal politics interfere with this privacy. One way the Mashantucket Pequot Tribe has maintained privacy is to designate a specific individual to handle the claims of tribal members and employees working in the same department.

12. While the health care industry can offer meaningful employment for tribal members, most jobs are relatively low-paying, high-stress data processing positions. For tribal members to work in higher-level professional jobs, they must invest in education and obtain the professional degrees and licenses.

13. Rapid growth is hard to manage. Get each step of growth stabilized before adding more programs or volume. Growth must occur in concert with revenues and investments. The TPA cannot allow a backlog of claims to create so much pressure to pay claims that they are not reviewed adequately.

14. It takes time to build a successful managed care enterprise. Expect it to take longer and cost more than your numbers suggest. The return on investments in health services is not as high as gaming, and it takes longer to see a profit. To become fully functional can take five years. Experience is a great teacher!

Chapter 6
Summary

Like the Blind Men and the Elephant, each of the case studies in this report are different in some ways. The organizations represent different parts of the Indian health spectrum. Chief Andrew Isaac Health Center is operated under a compact, services to the Pascua Yaqui Tribe are managed by the Indian Health Service, the Indian Health Board of Minneapolis is an urban Indian clinic, and the Mashantucket Pequot Tribal Nation offers health services through tribally generated funds plus a contract with the IHS.

These cases are also different because the Indian organizations are assuming different roles in relation to managed care. Chief Andrew Isaac Health Center and the Indian Health Board of Minneapolis are the providers. The Indian Health Service is the purchaser in both the Chief Andrew Isaac Health Center model and the Pascua Yaqui Health Plan. The Mashantucket Pequot Tribe is both purchaser, plan, consumer, and provider of pharmaceutical services.

The context of managed care also differs in these case
studies. Chief Andrew Isaac Health Center illustrates many
of the principles of managed care even though it is operating in a state which does not have a managed care environment. Both the Pascua Yaqui Tribe and the Indian Health
Board of Minneapolis are in states where the Medicaid program is managed care and this is an important element in
shaping their health care delivery systems. The Pequot Tribe,
is a large employer using managed care as a way to control
the costs of employee health benefits.

Because of these differences, the different Indian organizations view managed care in different ways. While contracts
define the relationships within a network of providers in a
plan, it is very different to be the provider rather than the
plan. When the Indian Health Board of Minneapolis receives
a contract from a plan, they can decide to "take it or leave
it," but they feel powerless to negotiate rates and terms which
will make it more feasible for them to provide services to
Medicaid recipients. On the other side of the spectrum is the
Mashantucket Pequot Tribe which is the owner and administrator of a plan that drafts contracts and sends them to providers, telling them to "take it or leave it."

To highlight these differences, each of these case studies
focuses on different aspects. The Chief Andrew Isaac Health
Center case study has more information about patient care,
while the case study about the Indian Health Board of Minneapolis has more information about contractual relation-

ships. Financial relationships and risk are explored to a greater extent in the Pascua Yaqui case study. The case study of the Mashantucket Pequot Tribal Nation has a more "how to" approach with a focus on benefit package and management of services. Taken together, the four case studies are intended to illustrate that managed care is about both managing patients and managing money.

While each of these cases is different, they also share some common features. All of the cases illustrate the interrelationship between the components of managed care and the application of the basic principles of managed care.

Components of Managed Care

Managed care has four essential components: a purchaser, a plan, providers, and consumers.

Purchaser

The purchaser pays for the plan on behalf of the consumers. In the Chief Andrew Isaac and Pascua Yaqui case studies, the purchaser is the Indian Health Service. The state Medicaid managed care program is the purchaser in the case study of the Indian Health Board of Minneapolis. The Mashantucket Pequot Tribe purchases the health plan for its tribal members and employees.

Plan

The health plan is both an organization and a document that defines benefits, costs, and rules for members. The

Pascua Yaqui Health Plan and the Mashantucket Pequot
Health Benefit Plan are two examples of the plan as a document defining benefits, costs, and rules for members. In the
case of the Indian Health Board of Minneapolis, there are
several Medicaid managed care health plans with essentially the same benefits defined by the state. However, each
plan has different rules for members that define the network of providers they may use.

As an organization, the plan serves as an intermediary
between the purchaser, the providers, and consumers. The
plan receives money from the purchaser and uses it to pay
the providers for services to the consumers. Managing
money is the main goal of the plan. To manage money, the
plan develops contractual relationships with providers. Volume purchasing allows the plan to negotiate discounted rates
with providers. Contractual relationships define a network
of providers within the plan.

In the case studies, the plan for Chief Andrew Isaac Health
Center is managed by Tanana Chiefs Conference, Inc. Southwest Catholic Health Network manages the plan for the
Pascua Yaqui Tribe. The Mashantucket Pequot Tribe manages its own plan. And there are four different health plans
contracting with the Indian Health Board of Minneapolis.

Providers

Providers are physicians, hospitals, laboratories, physical therapists, home health care agencies, pharmacies, and

others who provide health services. Providers deliver health services to consumers. Providers contract with health plans to receive payment for consumers who are enrolled in those plans. Plans usually limit providers to referring patients to other providers within the network of the plan. A primary care provider is usually assigned to each consumer when they enroll in the plan. The primary care provider is usually responsible for managing the patient's care.

In these case studies, the primary care provider organizations are Chief Andrew Isaac Health Center, El Rio Health Center for the Pascua Yaqui Health Plan, and the Indian Health Board of Minneapolis. The Mashantucket Pequot Health Benefit Plan does not require plan members to enroll with primary care providers and consumers may select their providers from the private sector with incentives for using the PPO network.

Consumers

Consumers enroll in health plans. As members of a health plan, they are entitled to the benefits defined by the plan. When they seek services from a provider in the network according to the rules of the plan, the plan will pay for those services. In these case studies, the consumers for Chief Andrew Isaac Health Center and Pascua Yaqui are tribal members who are eligible for the Indian Health Service. The consumers that are the focus of the case study of the Indian Health Board of Minneapolis are people who are receiving Medicaid in Hennepin County. For the Pequot case study, the consumers are tribal members and tribal employees and their dependents.

Common Features of Managed Care

Managed care includes a variety of approaches for organizing the delivery of health services. This report has identified, defined and illustrated eight common features of managed care:

1. A health plan defines benefits and limitations for the consumer at a fixed annual cost.
2. Health care providers are part of networks organized by health plans and defined by their contractual relationships with the plan.
3. Primary care providers are generally paid a fixed amount for each patient assigned to their care.
4. Financial risk usually is shared by the providers.
5. Total risk is limited through reinsurance or stop-loss plans.
6. Case management, preadmission screening, utilization review, formularies and copayments are used to provide services most economically.
7. Costs are controlled through a variety of measures, such as discounts in contracts with providers and group purchasing through networks.
8. Quality assurance programs are required to assure that needed care is delivered in a timely way, that consumers are satisfied with the services, and that prevention measures are provided.

The first case study of Chief Andrew Isaac Health Center (CAIHC) was intended to make people feel comfortable with the concepts of managed care because they are very similar to features which are already part of the delivery of Indian health services. Like managed care organizations, CAIHC has defined benefits and limitations which are provided at a fixed annual cost. Health care providers belong to networks defined by contractual relationships. The basis for funding for primary care is more closely related to user population size than to the number of services delivered. TCC assumes financial risk, although total risk is limited through reinsurance or stop-loss plans, including CHEF and ANMC. Case management, preadmission screening, utilization review, and a formulary are used to provide services in the most economical way. Costs are controlled through a variety of measures, such as discounts in contracts with providers and group purchasing through networks. Quality assurance programs assure that needed care is delivered in a timely way, that consumers are satisfied with the services, and that prevention measures are provided.

The concept that health care providers are part of networks organized by health plans and defined by contractual relationships is illustrated from the provider perspective by the case study of the Indian Health Board of Minneapolis, and from the plan perspective by the case study of the Pequot Tribe. In general, each provider is networked to several plans. And each plan has a network of many providers. A diagram of these relationships would look like a spider web.

The Pascua Yaqui case study is the only one in this series that illustrates the concept of primary care providers paid a fixed amount for each patient assigned to their care and assuming financial risk. The El Rio Health Center is paid on a capitated basis. It assumes financial risk for outpatient care. Both the Indian Health Board of Minneapolis and the Pequot Tribe case studies have essentially a fee-for-service system to pay providers at contracted rates. However, the MPHBP does assume risk as a plan and does reinsure to protect itself.

Quality of Care

Because the Indian Health Service is funded at a level well below the need, people often assume that the quality of care is compromised by the lack of resources. However, these four case studies demonstrate a quality of care that likely exceeds that of most managed care or fee-for-service organizations.

All of the organizations in these case studies that are eligible to apply for accreditation by the Joint Commission on Accreditation of Health Care Organizations (JCAHO) have received that accreditation. Chief Andrew Isaac Health Center has received accreditation with commendation, the highest level of accreditation. JCAHO accreditation standards emphasize quality assurance. Furthermore, HEDIS measures, that have become the standard for the managed care industry are used to measure quality in the Pascua Yaqui Health Plan and the Indian Health Board of Minneapolis.

The Indian health organizations in these case studies have gone far beyond these standard approaches to quality assurance. They have developed innovative ways to make sure that consumers receive the health care that they need.

Unlike most private health care systems in which consumers must initiate the process of receiving care by making appointments, the case management programs at CAIHC identify high-risk patients and track their care to assure that there is appropriate followup. Something as common as an annual Pap smear is given scrutiny to assure that all abnormal findings are followed by the next level of intervention. The results of this intensive case management have been a reduction in the number of cases of invasive carcinoma. While one of the incentives and rewards to the organization for this type of case management is lower health care costs, the consumer also receives a higher quality of care.

The Mashantucket Pequot Tribe has developed an innovative approach for assuring quality of care in their dental plan. The health plan will not pay dental bills until the dentist that performed the work submits an X-ray of the completed work. A dentist working for the health plan reviews the X-ray to assure that the work was necessary and that it was completed properly. This has reduced the amount of unnecessary work and fraudulent charges, thus saving the plan money. At the same time, it has improved the quality of care by making dentists more accountable, providing peer review, and eliminating incompetent dentists from the network of providers under the plan.

Most of the providers in these case studies are culturally sensitive, and traditional medical practices are encouraged. In addition, the Tribes have developed ways to improve consumer satisfaction with services. The Pascua Yaqui Tribe has two tribal members who serve as patient advocates, one located at the El Rio Health Center and one on the reservation. These patient advocates work to resolve any problems that consumers may have with their health care. At the Mashantucket Pequot Tribal Clinic the physicians serve as patient advocates for tribal members served under the health plan. They help patients understand their diagnosis and treatment with private physicians under the health plan. They even make home visits and accompany tribal members to surgery.

Native American consumers served in these case studies have access to modern facilities, state-of-the-art equipment, and medical specialists. While these things are expected by most consumers in the United States, they are not always found in Indian Health Service settings.

In the tribal programs that have evolved from Indian Health Service programs, there is an emphasis on prevention, including people who are specially trained and designated to provide prevention services. At CAIHC, for example, there is a patient educator, a nutritionist, and an immunization coordinator. There are also public health nurses, community health representatives, and community health educators.

These types of positions and responsibilities for prevention activities are not usually found in private sector settings.

It has been said that if the IHS were fully funded, it would be the best managed care organization in the world. In three of the case studies, the level of federal funding is a problem. The internal policies and programs developed by these organizations to manage care and manage costs have enabled these organizations to provide more services on a limited budget. However, as Indian health providers increasingly rely on third-party revenues, payments through managed care plans are further squeezing the resources available to serve an ever growing population. Waiting times for appointments is one indicator of lack of resources, as well as an indicator of quality of care. In one of the cases, waiting time was perceived as a problem by consumers.

Consensus Recommendations from All Case Studies

The following recommendation emerged as a consensus from all of the case studies. They were offered by people in leadership and management roles from the perspectives of purchasers, plans, and providers.

Planning is essential. Before beginning new programs, do a cost-benefit analysis. Remember that you cannot be all things for all people, so you have to be selective about the programs you provide. Identify needs and opportunities. Do feasibility studies. Target the market you are seeking to penetrate. Be flexible and creative in designing systems. Use a team approach so that you get many perspectives. Decide what the Tribe can do successfully and what services and expertise the Tribe needs to obtain through contracts with other organizations. If you have the opportunity to negotiate Medicaid managed care contracts, get as much information as you can about state-mandated benefits and your own costs for providing services.

Leadership of Indian health programs must stay involved at the state, and national levels. It is essential for Indian health programs to monitor trends and external forces at the federal, state and county levels. Chief Executive Officers must hire the best people they can find to take care of the day-to-day operations, so that leadership can focus on networking outside the organization and learning about trends in the larger environment. It is important to participate in the planning at the state level and to influence the decisions that shape the program. This participation can be through associations or lobbyists. Find tribal members with health knowledge to serve on the board of directors of tribal health enterprises. Tribal leaders need to be informed and need to keep tribal members informed.

Hire people for management positions with experience in both the private sector and Indian health. Start with experienced staff rather than trusting consultants to design processes and train staff. Hire people who have expertise in both the private health system and the federal government. It is important to know the federal system to make it work for you. People in key positions with experiences outside the Indian Health Service (I/T/U) system make them aware of different ways of approaching problem solving. Look for people with multiple professional and technical skills, including health care, finance, and computers. Seek people able to balance patient needs with financial resources. Managers need to embrace a team approach. Shared responsibility for developing policies that balance costs with needs for patient care, such as the formulary or the rules that govern referrals to specialists, lead to shared responsibility for carrying out those decisions.

Purchasing computer hardware and software is one of the major investments needed to compete in the managed care market place. The data systems offered by the IHS, such as RPMS, do not meet the needs of managed care. Tribes will have to find data systems to meet their particular needs. Managed care systems require a huge investment in technology and learning how to use it. Do your homework. Don't just listen to one approach. Everyone seems to be selling their goods or services—they embellish the good and don't tell you the bad aspects of their products. Companies will always try to sell you the most sophisticated software on the market—you need to question the application and workflow. When purchasing goods or services from consultants or vendors, ask for a list of their clients. Don't let them steer you to a happy client they have selected. Interview clients whose operations are similar to yours, and go look at their operations. Because technology changes so rapidly, the Tribe must keep investing in replacement technology, upgrading equipment and training. As computer needs change, it is important to consider using a single platform so that systems can be integrated. Do not buy software with capability beyond your needs.

Find mentors and role models. It is difficult to know who to trust for advice. Consultants tend to be self-serving and costly. If you are going to start a program, try to visit other similar programs to see how their systems are organized. This is difficult because they may view you as a competitor. However, if you tell them that you are only going to serve Indian populations, they may be more receptive to sharing information with you. The Tribes often are happy to share their experience and knowledge with other Tribes.

Develop long-term relationships based on good communications, problem solving, and trust. The purchaser, managed care plan, and providers should be considered partners in a long-term relationship. It is important to find a good partner, one who shares your philosophy and beliefs, who has experience dealing with similar populations, and who is culturally sensitive. It takes at least three years to identify and resolve problems. Organizations should not be judged on their initial performance, but rather on their efforts to make improvements to get things to run smoothly. For this reason, the first contract should be at least a three-year contract. Regular meetings between the contractor, the provider, and the Tribe are very helpful. Pay attention to things beyond finance. The Tribe or IHS should not just be a purchaser of health care; they must become a part of the system. This means that management should attend meetings, work to solve problems, and advocate for patient needs. Providers should not regard managed care plans as the enemy. If you know what you need, you can ask them for help. If they cannot increase their capitation or fee-for-service rates, they may be able to provide some services in kind. For example, they may be able to donate computers.

If you want to make money in managed care, you have to enroll people while they are healthy. Programs that depend on Medicaid managed care income must assure that Indian people are enrolled in health plans for which the Indian health program is a provider. If state or county social services are the only place that Medicaid recipients can enroll in health plans, then it is essential that people working in these agencies know about Indian health programs and that they have the information to educate Indian consumers about managed care options. Indian health programs can't survive the way they were. They must change to become more customer-centered to compete with other clinics. Hospitality is important.

Managing care involves managing costs. Managing costs can take several forms, such as focusing on prevention, providing services in the least costly setting, and reducing unnecessary services. Most strategies for managing costs include combining purchasing power of different organizations to create sufficient volume to be able to negotiate lower prices. In the CAIHC case study, considerable savings were achieved by using the military purchasing system. If you need to reduce costs, consider the following strategies: Can you subcontract services for less cost? Can you piggyback with others for more purchasing clout for such things as supplies and telephone service? Can you reduce costs through technology? Can you share staffing with another organization for such things as human resource department? Can you increase your productivity (number of visits per provider per day)?

Additional Recommendations for Purchasing a Managed Care Plan

1. Involve the Tribe in every step of the process from the beginning. Tribal members need to be educated about how managed care works and how to use the system effectively.

2. Don't contract with the lowest bidder on the basis of cost alone.

3. The contract should specify expectations about quality management, utilization management and long term community health objectives.

Additional Recommendations for Starting a Managed Care Plan

1. A Dental PPO is a good place to start a managed care enterprise. It is less complicated than a Medical PPO, it does not require big investments in computers, and it takes only a few employees to manage claims. The Dental PPO should be under the direction of dentist who can relate to other dentists in the private sector. A dental assistant who understands terms can be trained to handle claims. The most effective way to save money for clients is to demand that dental work be completed before payment by reviewing final X-rays. In organizing a Dental PPO, you must be fair to dentists, but watch what they do!

2. If you are starting a TPA and taking over claims management from another business, negotiate the conditions of the transition. Don't just end the previous plan without defining how claims received but not paid will be handled.

3. Customer service is important to keep consumers, providers and clients happy. The most knowledgeable employees, who have worked as claims adjusters, should be assigned to customer service. By scanning claims, all information is available in computer files and most decisions can be made on the first telephone call without requiring any return calls.

4. Maintain the privacy of clients and consumers–do not let tribal politics interfere with this privacy. One way the Mashantucket Pequot Tribe has maintained privacy is to designate a specific individual to handle the claims of tribal members and employees working in the same department.

5. While the health care industry can offer meaningful employment for tribal members, most jobs are relatively low-paying, high-stress data processing positions. For tribal members to work in higher level professional jobs, they must invest in education and obtain the professional degrees and licenses.

6. Rapid growth is hard to manage. Get each step of growth stabilized before adding more programs or volume. Growth must occur in concert with revenues and investments. The TPA cannot allow a backlog of claims to create so much pressure to pay claims that they are not reviewed adequately.

7. It takes time to build a successful managed care enterprise. Expect it to take longer and cost more than your numbers suggest. The return on investments in

health services are not as high as gaming and it takes longer to see a profit. To become fully functional can take 5 years. Experience is a great teacher!

The Future of Managed Care in Indian Health

Although the federal government is no longer pursuing an agenda of national health care reform, at least 44 state governments have changed their Medicaid programs to managed care and the Medicare program is rapidly developing managed care options for beneficiaries. More than 70 percent of all employees with health benefits in the United States are enrolled in managed care plans. There is no doubt that managed care will be the dominant organizational structure for health care in America in the future.

Managed care is continually changing and reinventing itself in creative and complex ways. The basic principles explored in these case studies are likely to remain the foundation for innovations, but a whole new vocabulary is emerging to describe variations. Terms like "variable cost risk pool," "private label HMOs," "direct access care systems," and "shadow capitation" speak to the complexity of new concepts in managed care.

In general, managed care is moving towards giving consumers more choices, giving providers less pay, and giving health plans more power. Consumers are attracted to plans which give them choice and these are becoming more competitive in the marketplace. Purchasers, both employers and government, to want to reduce capitation rates. At the same time, as health plans increasingly become profit-making enterprises, they have a greater expectation to return a profit to investors. Both of these trends put pressure on health plans to reduce their payments to providers. As capitation rates decline, there is a trend toward larger and fewer health plans. This could be considered "survival of the fittest" in an environment of intense competition. At the same time, the more market share that a health plan has, the greater the risk pool and the greater the likelihood of making money.

What does this mean for Tribes and urban Indian programs? In this environment, bigger is better. At the present time, managed care is moving toward bigger systems while the Indian Health Service is being divided into smaller health care delivery systems. Market forces mean that bigger organizations have better negotiating and purchasing power than smaller organizations. If Tribes can find better forms of cooperation between departments within their tribal operations (such as employee health benefits and tribal health services), with other Tribes, and with other types of organizations, they will be more competitive in the current managed care environment.

In places where managed care is slow to develop, Tribes may have a competitive advantage because they are already familiar with the concepts of managed care as practiced through Indian health systems. Some observers say that the system of tribally operated health services may form an HMO in Alaska. A statewide HMO of Alaska Native health providers would provide a mechanism to reintegrate a health care delivery system which has experienced fragmentation as a result of P.L. 93-638 contracting and compacting. At the present time this is purely speculative, but the foundation is there for future development.

Just as each of these case studies is different, every Tribe is in an environment with unique opportunities and challenges. These case studies are intended to help Tribes visualize some of the ways that managed care can be further developed to meet their specific tribal needs. Through these case studies, those working outside American Indian and Alaska Native communities may better understand the challenges of integrating the complex Indian health care delivery system into managed care.

People Interviewed for this Report

Case 1:
Chief Andrew Isaac Health Center (CAIHC)

Dan Adams, RN, *Quality Assurance Director, CAIHC*

Marjorie Allan, RN, *ANP, CAIHC*

James Armbrust, *Director, Offices of Regional & Contract Health, Alaska Area, IHS*

Beverly Beardsley, *Director, Medical Records, CAIHC*

Jonah Bolt, *Business Office, Tanana Chiefs Conference*

Russ Cox, *Assistant Administrator, Fairbanks Memorial Hospital*

Charlotte Davis, RN, *Elder Care Coordinator, CAIHC*

Ron Davis, *Administrator, Tanana Valley Clinic*

Cheryl Denton, LPN, *Pap Coordinator, CAIHC*

Merlan O. Ellis, RN, *Director Contract Health Services, CAIHC*

Judi Flory, RN, *Patient Educator, CAIHC*

Donna Galbreath, MD, *CAIHC*

Marilyn Harasick, RN, *Health Center Director,* CAIHC

Wade Henry, *Director, Division of Contract Health Services, Alaska Area,* IHS

Josephine Huntington, *Assistant Director for Compacting, Tanana Chiefs Conference*

William James, MD, *Medical Director,* CAIHC

James Kohler, LTC, *Deputy Commander for Administration, Bassett Army Hospital*

Eileen Kozevinkoff, *Health Services Director, Tanana Chiefs Conference*

Elaine Landon, *Health Services Administration Director, Tanana Chiefs Conference*

Josephine Malemute, RN, *Clinical Nursing Director,* CAIHC

Dave Mather, Ph.D., *Mather and Associates*

Cyndi Nation-Cruikshank, *Home Health Care Coordinator,* CAIHC

Roger Nicolaus, RPh, *Director of Pharmacy,* CAIHC

Mike Powers, *Administrator, Fairbanks Memorial Hospital*

Walter Palkovitch, RN, *Community Health Nursing Director*

Dave Schraer, MD, *Deputy Director, Alaska Area,* IHS

Case 2:
Pascua Yaqui Tribe (PYT)

Cathy Cordova, QA/UR *Analyst, Office of Health Planning,* PYT

Maria Cruz, *Director, Health Department,* PYT

Kristobal Fimbres, *Patient Advocate,* PYT

Rojelia Gallardo, *Community Member*

Delores Garcia, *Data Processing Technician, Office of Health Planning, PYT*

Robert Gomez, *Executive Director, El Rio Health Center*

Sally Gonzales, *Tribal Council Member and Health Plan Advisory Board Member, PYT*

Lydia Goudeau, *CHR Supervisor, Health Department, PYT*

Liz Guerra, *Project Officer, Tucson Area, IHS*

John Kitteredge, MD, *Chief Medical Officer, Tucson Area, IHS*

Rebecca Martinez, *Office Manager, Office of Health Planning, PYT*

Anna Molina, *Community Member*

Tula McCarthy, RN, *Director of Nursing, Health Department, PYT*

David Ramirez, *Chairman, Health Plan Advisory Board, PYT*

Jack Ramirez, *Health Plan Manager, PYT*

Rebecca Tapia, *Health Plan Advisory Board, PYT*

Julie Trepeda, *Chief Operating Officer, Southwest Catholic Health Network*

Case 3:
Indian Health Board of Minneapolis

Eric D. Anderson, *Planning Director, Minnesota Department of Human Services*

Lydia Caros, MD, *Medical Director, Indian Health Board of Minneapolis*

Joan Delich, *Director, Administrative Services, Metropolitan Health Plan*

Shelly Garcia, *Allina Health Plan*

Doug Henson, *Director of Customer Relations, Hennepin County Medical Center*

Carol Marquez, *Indian Health Board of Minneapolis*

Angie McCollum, *Health Care Compliance Specialist, Minnesota Department of Human Services*

Kris McKean, *Billing Coordinator, Indian Health Board of Minneapolis*

Christine Roy, *Indian Advocate, Hennepin County Medical Center*

Virginia Schuster, *Clinic Administrator, Indian Health Board of Minneapolis*

Norine Smith, *Executive Director, Indian Health Board of Minneapolis*

Case 4:
Mashantucket Pequot Tribal Nation (MPTN)

Angela Bishop, *Acting Vice President for Third Party Administration (TPA), Pequot Pharmaceutical Network (PRxN), MPTN*

Dawn Coley, *Vice President for Employee Health Services, PRxN, MPTN*

Kara Hatch, *Network Manager, PRxN, MPTN*

Dawn M. Hazard, *Contract Health Services Administrator, Health Department, MPTN*

Larry Holder, *Vice President for MIS, PRxN, MPTN*

Kathy Doubleday, *Case Manager, TPA Division, MPTN*

George M. McMullen, *Coordinator of Planning, PRxN, MPTN*

William A. Millar, II, RPh, *CEO/President, PRxN, MPTN*

Karen Pont, *Patient Services Coordinator, Health Department, MPTN*

Amarillys Rodriguez, MD, *Medical Director, Health and Human Services Department, MPTN*

William Siemiaszko, DDS, *Dental Plan Director, TPA Division, PRxN, MPTN*

Michael Sockalexis, *Administrative Planning Supervisor, Health and Human Services Department, MPTN*

Beth Thomas, *Acting Health Director, Health Department, MPTN*

Phyllis Monroe Waite, *Chairperson, PRxN Board of Directors, MPTN*

JoAnn Zingoni, RPh, *Vice President of Pharmacy Operations, PRxN, MPTN*

Glossary of Terms[8]

Capitated Payments Charges for health care services based on a per person charge for all services rendered over a fixed period of time (usually monthly or yearly).

Capitation A precalculated dollar amount paid to a provider or insurer to cover the cost of all health care services delivered per person over a specified period of time (usually monthly or yearly).

Case Management A patient-specific process, involving individualized assessments of service needed and provision of assistance to individuals in obtaining specific services. In Medicaid managed care, case management usually means gatekeeping (preauthorization) patients' access to covered Medicaid specialty services.

---

[8]Definitions in this glossary were developed by the staff of the Oklahoma Health Care Authority in 1994 and modified by NIHB for this report.

Copayment   An amount which the member pays directly to a provider or health plan at the time covered services are rendered.

Enrollment   The process by which a person who has been determined eligible to receive benefits becomes a member of a health plan.

Fee-for-Service Reimbursement   The traditional health care payment system under which physicians and other providers receive payment for each unit of service provided. Payment occurs after the service (retrospectively).

Formulary   A listing of prescription medications which are approved for use and/or coverage by a health plan and which will be dispensed through participating pharmacies to a covered person.

Gatekeeper   Primary care provider, who is primarily responsible for all medical treatment rendered, makes referrals as necessary and monitors the patient's treatment.

Health Care Financing Administration (HCFA)   The organization within the U.S. Department of Health and Human Services that has responsibility for administering Medicare and the federal participation in Medicaid.

Health Maintenance Organization (HMO)   An entity that provides, offers or arranges for coverage of designated health services needed by plan members for a fixed, pre-paid premium. Under the Federal HMO Act, an entity must have the following three characteristics to call itself an HMO: an organized system for providing health care or otherwise assuring health care delivery in a geographic area; an agreed upon set of basic and supplemental health maintenance and treatment services; and a voluntary enrolled group of people.

Health Plan   A network of health care providers which is capable of delivering comprehensive health care services that meet a required set of basic benefits, often including inpatient and outpatient services, mental health services, and preventive services. A health plan may be an affiliation of both providers and insurers.

Incurred But Not Reported (IBNR) Claims   Liability for services rendered for which claims have not been received.

Indian Health Service (IHS)   A division of the U.S. Public Health Service in the Department of Health and Human Services that administers a health care delivery system for American Indians and Alaska Natives enrolled in federally recognized tribes.

Indemnity   An insurance program in which the insured person is reimbursed for covered expenses.

Integrated Service Delivery Network   A network of health care providers which is capable of delivering comprehensive health care services that meet a required set of basic benefits, often including inpatient and outpatient services, mental health services and preventive services. An integrated service delivery network may be an affiliation of providers and insurers.

Managed Care   Groups of health care providers who participate in networks in which providers have incentives to assure appropriate and cost-effective service delivery, to reduce unnecessary procedures, and to achieve some uniformity of medical procedures and practice. Providers within the networks are usually compensated by capitated payments or by fees which are discounted. The most common managed care systems are Health Maintenance Organizations (HMOs), which usually provide coverage to plan members for a fixed, prepaid premium, and Preferred Provider Organizations (PPOs), which usually provide coverage at discounted fees with reduced copayments to members receiving services within the provider network.

Medicaid   A federal/state program authorized by Title XIX of the Social Security Act, as amended, which provides federal matching funds for a medical assistance program for recipients of federally aided public assistance, Supplemental Security Income (SSI) and other specified groups. The federal government defines the minimum populations and services to be included; however, states may add populations and services at state expense.

Medicare   A federal health insurance program, established by Title XVIII of the Social Security Act, for people who are over age 65, or disabled, or receiving treatment for end-stage renal disease.

Preferred Provider Organization (PPO)   A program in which contracts are established with providers of medical care, and patients are given financial incentives to seek services from these providers.

Primary Care Provider (PCP) An individual responsible for the general medical care of a patient and the management of the patient's health care that includes, but is not necessarily limited to: a physician who is a family practitioner, general practitioner, pediatrician, or general internist.

Provider Any individual or group that provides a health care service, such as a physician, physician's assistant, nurse practitioner, midwife, therapist, hospital, group practice, nursing home, or pharmacy.

Quality Assurance Activities related to setting standards for care, measuring processes and outcomes that indicate the quality of care, and adjusting health care delivery systems and approaches to improve results.

Reinsurance Insurance purchased by an HMO, insurance company, or self-funded employer from another insurance company to protect itself against all or part of the losses that may be incurred in the process of honoring the claims of its participating providers, policy holders, or employees and covered dependents. Also called stop-loss insurance.

Section 1915b Medicaid Waiver Allows the Health Care Financing Administration to waive certain requirements under Section 1902 of the Medicaid Act, allowing states to limit choices of Medicaid consumers and to implement managed care in their Medicaid systems.

Section 1115 Medicaid Waiver   Allows the Health Care Financing Administration to waive certain requirements under Section 1902 of the Medicaid Act so that states can implement a statewide demonstration project of managed care.

Staff Model HMO   Health care system employing physicians to provide services to members. All premiums and other revenues accrue to the HMO, which compensates physicians by salary and incentive programs.

Stop-Loss Insurance   Coverage purchased by a health plan or self-funded employer to provide protection from losses resulting from claims over a specific dollar amount per member per year. There are two types of stop-loss insurance: specific or individual, and aggregate. In specific or individual insurance, reimbursement is given for claims on any covered individual which exceed a predetermined deductible such as $25,000 or $50,000. Aggregate insurance reimburses claims in which the total exceeds a predetermined level, such as 125 percent of the amount expected in an average year.

Utilization   The extent to which the patients use a program or obtain a particular service, or category of procedures, over a given period of time.

Utilization Management   The process of evaluating the necessity, appropriateness and efficiency of health care services. A utilization review coordinator gathers information about the proposed hospitalization, service or procedure from the patient and/or provider, then determines whether it meets established guidelines and criteria.

Utilization Review (UR) A formal review of patient utilization or of the appropriateness of health care services, on a prospective, concurrent, or retrospective basis.

Index

About the Author

Mim Dixon, a Policy Analyst for the National Indian Health Board (NIHB), has seven years of management experience in a tribally-operated health care program, and a wide range of policy and program development experience. She was the project coordinator for the State Managed Care Models project, author of the report, "Indian Health in Nine State Medicaid Managed Care Programs," and has co-authored a number of studies relating to Indian health care delivery systems. Her academic training is in economics (BA, Washington University) and anthropology (PhD, Northwestern University).

She served as a member of the American Public Health Association National Arctic Health Science Policy Task Force, co-chair of the Arctic Social Science Committee for the Polar Research Board of the National Research Council, advisor to the US Arctic Research Commission, and a member of the Center for Substance Abuse Prevention Workgroup on Managed Care and Behavioral Health. She received the prestigious Barbara Berger Award from the Alaska Public Health Association in 1991.